meditative
spaces

meditative
spaces

meditative
spaces

michael
freeman

UNIVERSE

First published in the United States of America in 2005 by UNIVERSE PUBLISHING
A Division of Rizzoli International Publications, Inc.
300 Park Avenue South, New York, NY 10010
www.rizzoliusa.com

Pages 72–73: photographs © Syu Htakeyama
Pages 164-165: photograph © Mikio Kurokawa
All other photographs and text © 2005 Michael Freeman

2005 2006 2007 2008 2009 / 10 9 8 7 6 5 4 3 2 1
Printed in China
ISBN: 0-7893-1353-7
Library of Congress Catalog Control Number: 2005902952
Japanese consultant and writer: Noriko Sakai
Image post-production: Yukako Shibata
Design by Claudia Brandenburg, Language Arts

introduction

The German existentialist philosopher Martin Heidegger argued that we constantly need to learn how to dwell, and that this means understanding the relationship between space and ourselves. In his seminal essay *Building Dwelling Thinking*, he stressed that by building we create a location which in turn allows for a particular kind of space, and that "thinking itself belongs to dwelling in the same sense as building." This is as true for a room as Heidegger wrote for a house, and there is a strong case to be made for building a space that allows for thinking—specifically for contemplation, meditation, or daydreaming.

In calling this book *Meditative Spaces*, I want to broaden the definition. At the core is formal meditation, which most people rightly associate mainly with Zen, but a look at the history of meditation shows that this is not exclusively a Buddhist domain. In Western

religions it often has been linked with mysticism; in Islam too, in the dancing of Sufi sects. And with nothing whatsoever to do with religion, people have always drawn strength from periods of quiet reflection, using whatever techniques they have been able to find to calm the mind and open it to the world.

One important technique is creating the right conditions—essentially the space. One great Zen master recommended a big, noisy bridge, but anyone other than an adept needs a quiet place, and more than this, solitude—as the German poet Rainer Maria Rilke put it, to be "magnificently alone." To achieve this, there must inevitably be the action of closing off, and by erecting boundaries, whether of wood, stone, paper, or the imagination, these places are experiments in the dialectics of inside and outside. As we'll see, these explorations take many forms. In some, the space is sealed off in such a way that knowledge and memory of the exterior are driven away, hinting at, in the words of the French philosopher Jean Hyppolite, "alienation and hostility between the two." Other meditative spaces play with the ambiguity of outside and inside, allowing the surroundings to enter in one sense while keeping them at bay in other ways.

By this closing off and by the invariably small dimensions, such spaces are always intensely personal. In his book *The Poetics of Space*, French philosopher Gaston Bachelard considered them in the context of a house as "the centers of condensation of intimacy, where daydreams accumulate." As domains of intimacy, they then became places "in which psychic weight is dominant."

For a number of reasons, Japanese culture embodies the idea and practice of creating meditative spaces more than any other I can think of. Much of this comes from Zen, either directly from the practice of meditation or at one step removed through the "tea-ceremony room." *Chanoyu* is an offspring, as it were, of Zen, and it furnishes us here with some striking spaces. As a culture, a practice, chanoyu resists easy definition, even for the Japanese. The classic treatise on it, written in English in 1906 by Tenshin Okakura, is *The Book of Tea*, and he begins by famously calling it "a cult founded on the adoration of the beautiful among the sordid facts of everyday existence. . . . It is essentially a worship of the Imperfect, as it is a tender attempt to accomplish something possible in this impossible thing we know as life." This may or may not bring us nearer to understanding this strange and refined culture, nor is this the purpose of this book, but for us the importance of chanoyu is the room created especially for it. There is no satisfactory English translation, though it is usually called "tea-ceremony room" or "tea room." The first puts too much emphasis on ritual, the second suggests a superior kind of café. Nevertheless, the small room, dedicated to one purpose, is designed as a place where host and guest can contemplate "the art of life." In Okakura's words, "Not a color to disturb the tone of the room, not a sound to mar the rhythm of things, not a gesture to obtrude on the harmony, not a word to break the unity of the surroundings, all movements to be performed simply and naturally." More than this, the tea-ceremony room, being a dedicated space and one that reflects the personality of its builder and user, has attracted modern architects and designers. The new versions included here are very strong on individuality, and not all are used in a formal way. Many are used for a more personal form of contemplation.

Meditation of any kind is an intensely personal matter, and in many ways this book is a personal exploration. There are no formal parameters for the design and construction of such spaces, and no formulae. With all this individualism, it is hardly surprising that there is no taxonomy of meditative spaces, but for the purpose of this book I have composed four groupings. First there are the spaces which, through a rigorous simplicity, provide the ideal conditions for emptying the mind. Then there are spaces that work by making an often dramatic shift to the personal surroundings. These are followed by ones that focus the attention, either perceptually or toward a purpose. The fourth group is of spaces that are imbued with a natural energy, through location, associations and memories, or their geometry.

Finally, a warning. The modern meditative spaces that follow are all works of the creative imagination, by artists, designers, architects, and individuals. Their common goal is to alter perception and thought, and this is a complex matter of the interaction between the space and the person entering it. What you see here is not necessarily what the person who designed, built, or uses the space may see.

One of the prime functions of a meditative space is to seal off the huge amount of sensory input from the outside world—to remove the clutter of daily life. The direct way to this end is simplicity. This seems like a pragmatic, obvious solution, but with most of the spaces that follow there is an ulterior motive. Simplifying the design of the room is both a metaphor for emptiness and an aid for emptying the mind. There is a Zen saying that "Form is emptiness and the very emptiness is form," and according to this strictest, most formal method of meditation, the no-mind state where nothing exists is its correct posture. The idea of nothingness as an ideal state for the mind is echoed in the teachings of the thirteenth-century Christian mystic Meister Johannes Eckhart, influential in his day. And one of the ways of rendering the name of the tea-ceremony room in Chinese characters is "the abode of vacancy," conveying the Taoist theory of the all-containing and the infinite. "The tea room is absolutely empty," writes Tenshin Okakura, "except for what may be placed there to satisfy some aesthetic mood." A first step toward emptying the mind is emptying the space.

zen modern

One of the techniques of Zen is the use of space to help establish a frame of mind. In Mito, north of Tokyo, the 350-year-old Gion-ji temple continues to put this into practice with architectural changes. In 2004 it was decided to create a new entrance space that would symbolize vacancy, with an underlying theme of reticence and strength. Mikami Architects was engaged, and they settled on a construction of bare concrete and cypress. The wood softens the solidity and strength of the concrete, and the cypress tree is itself full of spiritual associations. The view shown here is from the steps marking the boundary where the material world is left behind; here visitors remove their shoes and enter the austere space. Two skylights, one narrow and the other broad, allow daylight to flood the far wall, and the gathering light at the end of the expanse beckons as the "Pure Land" of the Zen sect. On the left side of this view of the entrance, a door slides back to reveal a small room for individual meditation, with a floor-level, frosted-glass window.

facing page: A small side room is bare except for a shelf supporting a bronze statue of Amitabha Tathagata, one of the five Dhyani Buddhas, flanked by two guardians. **following pages:** Seen from the steps, the entrance space achieves an impression of emptiness and expanse greater than its 48-by-18 foot dimensions.

paper space

In the center of a store handling kimono and traditional Japanese accessories in the town of Takamatsu, the owner, Masahiro Hasui, wanted a quiet space to escape from the rush of daily business. Specifically, he wanted it to be a space in which he could practice *zazen*—the meditation technique unique to Zen. The architect, Tetsuo Goto, put into practice his principle of "subjectivity"—engineering the space from the inside looking out. In this case, his starting point was "what it might be like to be inside an Akari light" (the paper lanterns made famous by sculptor Isamu Noguchi, who lived and worked nearby).

Goto used shoji, the traditional screens made by stretching translucent paper over a light wooden frame, but he did so over the entire wall and ceiling area. He then fitted fifty fluorescent tubes in the 24-inch space between the shoji and wall, with dimmer controls so that not

right: This arrangement of the tatami blocks around the circumference is traditional for *zazen*, in which trainee Zen monks sit facing the wall. The shadows of the shoji crosspieces create a focus for concentration.

only can the overall level of brightness be adjusted, but also the balance between artificial light and the more concentrated daylight entering from three relatively small windows, one in each of three walls. Careful examination reveals considerable subtlety in the shoji application. There is a second paper layer that blurs the edges of the wooden crosspieces for a softer effect, and, the pattern of the crosspieces is different for each side. In the view here, the far wall faces

south, so that east, the direction of the rising sun, is on the left. For this left wall, the spacing is more open to gently acknowledge sunrise.

The flooring is covered with flag stones of local *yura-ishi* (a local green stone), for as we'll see on pages 142–145, this area is famous for stone and has bred generations of carvers and sculptors. On top of this are placed movable 35 x 35-inch tatami square blocks, which can be configured in different ways but are always arranged so

that the texture of the green *igusa* (the rush used to make tatami mats) alternates to give a checkerboard pattern. The overall effect is exactly that of inhabiting a glowing paper cube. There is yet one more local reference—"there is a tradition," explains Goto, "that in the past the ruler had a room with a paper ceiling and walls to make it difficult for ninja assassins to approach surreptitiously."

facing page: A combination of concealed fluorescent strip lights and daylight equally bathes the interior's ceiling and walls.
right: The entrance as seen from inside. Utilities are concealed behind white sliding screens. Immediately outside is the alcove featured on page 151.

above and facing page: The two
sources of light are fluorescent
strips (above) and daylight through
three windows (facing page), and
they can be utilized together. In
this arrangement, tatami blocks on
castors have been gathered to
make a raised floor.

right: A double thickness of hand-made paper softens the appearance of the wooden framework. The crosspieces make a point on which to focus and center the mind during meditation.

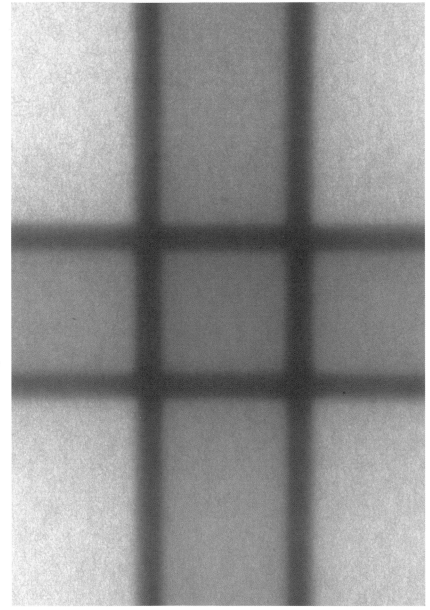

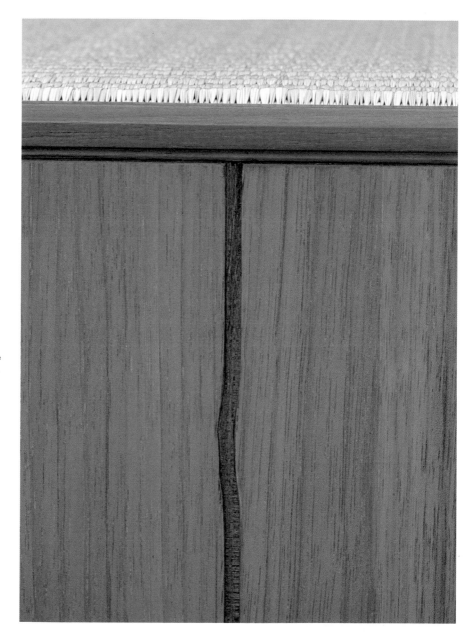

right: The blocks that carry the tatami squares have been painstakingly jointed to follow the natural irregularities of the wood.

oval space

The owner of the Takasu Kogei store in Takamatsu also commissioned a young architect, Shinji Kagawa, to design a different kind of meditation room. His concept for the five-story building was to create different interpretations of the Japanese spirit as a means of enhancing the sensibility of people coming to see his collection of kimono. The idea here is the protection and enclosure of the womb, and to this end Kagawa designed an oval space with soft lighting, natural colors, and walls plastered with diatomaceous earth. The detailing is impressive. The lighting for the most part is concealed behind screens and panels, while the central ceiling light filters through rolled Japanese paper that has been dyed with willow. Along one side is a low table by the acclaimed Japanese-American woodworker and furniture designer George Nakashima, who had active ties with local craftsmen. For the owner, Masahiro Hasui, the experience of this enclosing space is like "being in an oasis."

facing page: The gentle curve of the rolled-paper light diffusers echoes the curved walls of the oval room, divided by a crossbeam that carries sliding paper screens.
right: A detail of the ceiling light of rolled, dyed paper.

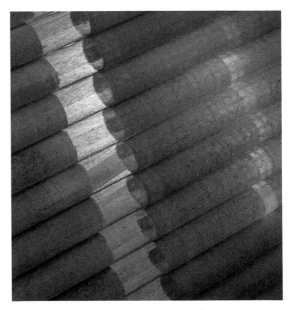

above: A low table by George Nakashima occupies the center of one half of the space, seen here with the screens open.

facing page: In the other direction, the visitor faces a huge curved wall of elegant simplicity, plastered with earth and with a tiny doorway that opens to an interior garden of cubic stones, decorated with a vase of camellia.

While the Sufi sects of Islam probably furnish the best-known examples of meditative dancing, in which a constantly repeated cycle of whirling, jumping, and rhythmic swaying induces an almost trance like state, the Shakers in eighteenth-century America also developed this form of meditation, from which their name is derived. Dancing worship, which became formalized and more orderly in the 1790s, took place in spacious, plain "meeting rooms," always spotless, polished, and stripped of unnecessary furniture or decoration.

far right: The meeting room of the Center Family in Pleasant Hill, Kentucky, with its coved roof and austere but bright color scheme.
right: The Meetinghouse interior at Sabbathday Lake in Maine, its exposed beams painted in the costly but traditional deep blue. The portable benches were moved aside for dance.

a painter's room

Painter and sculptor Tatsuhiko Yokoo moved his studio and home to the wooded hills of Chichibu, one of the sacred places for Japanese esoteric Buddhism, and asked architect Takao Fujiki for a design that would help create the right conditions for his work. Connecting with nature was important, but even more so was the concept of nothingness, which figures largely in Zen meditation. Yokoo practices this before painting and is at pains to dis-tinguish between empti-ness and nothingness, which accumulates energy. He also points to the teachings of the thirteenth-century theologian and mystic Meister Johannes Eckhart (Yokoo is Catholic), which include, "If God is to make something of you or in you, then you must first yourself become noth-ingness" and "You could not do better than to go where it is dark, that is, unconsciousness." Both painter and architect agreed on a simple and stoic interior, using bare concrete and black oil-stained wood. The double-height studio is on the ground floor, and above it an equally tall meditation room with a floor area of just 35.5 square feet occu-pying its own corner tower. The arrangement, accord-ing to the architect, was to "combine two structures made of concrete and wood so as to make energy flow and spiral upwards through the whole build-ing." The design of the room is directed toward "nothingness," the interior black, with a small window at ground level that gives a view of the hills and an even smaller one high above.

below: The meditation room is an almost independent structure at one end of the building, clad with black-stained planking.

right: The view from the floor-level entrance, reached by steps. Meditation practice often involves the placing of an object for focus, and in this case the painter chose the reproduction of an icon—not, he stresses, for any religious meaning.

room in shadows

In the basement of this Tokyo house designed by architect Michimasa Kawaguchi, the owner, a university professor, wanted a room that would have no obvious functional purpose, simply for quiet reflection. Kawaguchi is much in demand for his individual style with homes, in which he manages to capture a very particular Japanese sensibility toward space and light. In his essay *In Praise of Shadows*, the renowned Japanese novelist

Junichiro Tanizaki wrote, "our ancestors, forced to live in dark rooms, presently came to discover beauty in shadows, ultimately to guide shadows towards beauty's ends," and that ultimately "we do prefer a pensive luster." The entire house is lit softly and indirectly. Maple trees and a 16-foot-high black fence block direct sunlight; for the basement, Kawaguchi let in a deep light well, with polished natural concrete walls that catch just the north light.

facing page: The careful balance of lighting draws the eye out toward the small, subdued garden, alluding to the opening up of imaginative space.
right: While still wet on the walls, the thick plaster was whisked to create this highly textural, frothy effect.

The room looks onto its small courtyard garden through plate glass. In the interior he used one of his trademark techniques to further mute the illumination, staining the floorboards with black calligraphy ink. The walls are rendered with a plaster that has a deep, porous texture, which two low-wattage spots throw into relief. The space is both tactile and subdued, to give it an air of introspection.

32 **earth and paper**

Atsushi Kitagawara, the architect responsible for the remarkably austere empty cube on pages 72–73, built for his own house a tea-ceremony room that sidesteps tradition. Photographed for the first time here (though completed eight years ago), it is a quintessentially personal space for calming the mind through concentrating on the preparation and sharing of tea. Studied simplicity underlies the design. The walls are simply rendered in earth from a mountain in Shinshu and mixed with starch and straw (collected from farmers by Kitagawara himself). The tatami floor is also simplified, doing without the usual embroidered borders. Light enters from two sources: a carefully crumpled and shaped screen of handmade paper over the window, and folded lengths of paper pasted over bamboo sticks to modify the ceiling lights. There is no traditional hanging scroll painting; Kitagawara prefers to choose something that he thinks would be appropriate for a guest—in this instance, me, and so the display here is a work by his friend, the photographer Yuriko Takagi.

right: This simplicity of natural materials is characteristic of the *sukiya* style of tea-ceremony room, here in contemporary form.

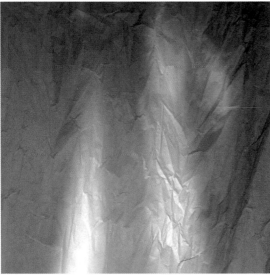

this page, clockwise from top left:
Broken stalks of straw were
mixed into the earth to render
arakabe walls; a leafy twig of
blueberry was chosen for this
autumn day; late afternoon
sunlight strikes the crumpled
paper covering the window.

facing page: A square hearth set
into the floor is for the iron kettle.
The long photograph against the
wall takes the place of a traditional
alcove display.
following pages: The ceiling is lined
with handmade paper that has
been folded and stuck to lengths of
bamboo by Kitagawara's students.

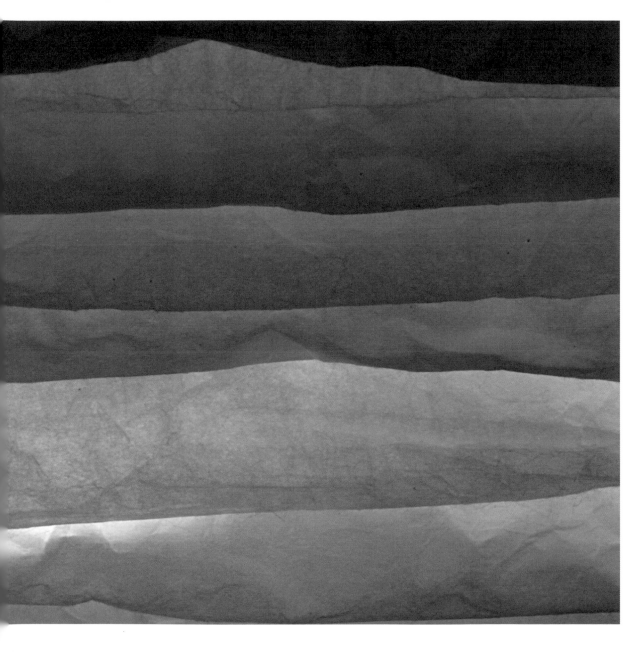

pebble pond

In a house in Osaka, architect Chitoshi Kihara and garden designer Yasujirou Aoki, who collaborate often, designed a modern tatami room that follows the *sukiya* style of natural materials and earthen colors, looking out onto a small rectangular garden. The plot, which can be flooded at will, is filled with pebbles and a stone basin for plants that are changed seasonally. The pond/garden takes the place of the traditional alcove (see pages 148–153) and its seasonally changing hanging scroll.

The dimness is intentional, to create a quiet and contemplative atmosphere that seems far from the surrounding city. It draws the eye outward to the restrained colors of the pebble pond, and allows the subtle invasions of daylight to be appreciated as the day unfolds. Novelist Junichiro Tanizaki, lover of shadows, wrote, "We delight in the mere sight of the delicate glow of fading rays clinging to the surface of a dusky wall, there to live out what little life remains to them." He continued, "Have you never felt a sort of fear in the face of the ageless, a fear that in that room you might lose all consciousness of the passage of time, that untold years might pass and upon emerging you should find you had grown old and gray?"

right: Rippling reflections of afternoon sunlight enter the darkened room from the surface of the pond.

the enigma of rocks

One Zen device for learning to see through to the reality of things is the koan, a seemingly nonsensical puzzle on which students meditate. Certain stone gardens are three-dimensional forms of koan; the most famous and enigmatic is at the Kyoto temple of Ryoan-ji. Creating gardens has long been an important way of practicing Zen, and in the medieval period Zen gardeners began to strip nature bare as a metaphor for discovering the true nature of the human being. The remaining essentials were rocks placed in a plain of raked gravel. Approximately five hundred years ago (the exact date, like much else about this garden, is unknown) a rectangular plot of about 2,100 square feet was laid out in this temple founded in 1450. Bound by a low clay wall on three sides, a raked bed of white gravel contains just fifteen stones, arranged in five groups— from right to left 3, 2, 3, 2, and 5.

There is a Zen term, *ishigokoro*, which means "reading the heart of a stone." As Shunmyo Masuno, Zen priest and the most respected contemporary designer of modern Zen gardens, says, it is essential "to explain the importance of stone in a Japanese garden, because it occupies a role not found in the West. Stones have a spiritual life as much as do plants and animals." How, then, to "read" Ryoan-ji? There have been many

interpretations, from mountain peaks protruding through a sea of clouds to a tigress helping its cubs swim across a river (a Chinese Han dynasty legend). Entire books have been written on this one concise stone garden and its possible meaning, but we should remember that Zen practice eschews understanding by applying the intellect, by using words and by acquiring scholastic knowledge. Understanding is based on transcendental insight, a direct leap "at the core of man" as one of its founding ancestors, Bodhidarma, wrote. And the special name for this garden is *mutei*, "garden of emptiness."

below: Of all the well-known dry-stone Zen gardens, the one at Ryoan-ji is the most minimal in its lack of spectacle. None of the fifteen stones dominates or is in any way distinctive.

simple stones

Stone has a primal role in meditation. According to Chinese and Japanese beliefs, stone is animate in the sense that it partakes of the mind-nature of all sentient beings. It has a spiritual existence, and Japanese Buddhism stresses that even insentient beings can expound the teachings. The view is not confined to the East. As translated by Graham Parkes, Goethe writes in *On Granite* that "the presence of rock brings elation and assurance to [his]

soul." Stones embody much to contemplate. In a restored wooden mansion that was once the home of a wealthy Yokohama merchant at the turn of the twentieth century, the gardens have been redesigned by Shunmyo Masuno. The theme is the Japanese spirit of receiving guests, and for one of the important rooms the Zen priest sited a single stone on each side, one naturally formed, the other carved to become a water basin resting on a polished black

slab. "Detail is of paramount importance," says Masuno, and this includes the wetting down of stones before a guest's arrival. "Also of importance is the guest's ability to recognize and appreciate all the detail paid."

right: The undulations of the natural folds in this metamorphic rock are echoed in the surrounding bed of moss. These waves make a deliberate contrast with the severe rectangular framing of the sliding screens.

right: In this arrangement, a large granite boulder (but with the pebblelike shape of a much smaller rock) has had a water basin chiseled into its upper surface. It rests on a black, flat stone base.

skip house

In a strange reinterpretation of Japanese domestic space, the Skip House in Kyoto has been designed by the architectural team FOBA with an uncompromisingly austere geometry, which in this simple room has been used to create a modern meditative space. Natural light filters down through a corner skylight and low porthole windows, mixing with recessed ceiling spotlights. Despite initial appearances, the elements *are* traditional, from the sliding shoji screens made of translucent handmade paper on frames to the tatami mats. Points of difference are that the room opens up on two sides completely and the mats are square and completely free of decoration. Color plays an essential part in this fusion of modern and traditional, with white as the background for dramatic interactions. Here, the interplay is between orange and green, and despite the seeming modernity of the combination, they too are traditional—the orange of Shinto shrines and torii gates, and the green of fresh *igusa* straw.

right: A sequence of orange-lit sliding paper screens runs in parallel grooves on two sides to open or enclose the simple, modern space.

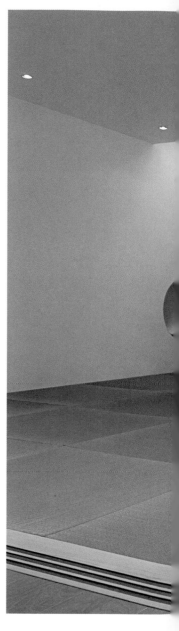

right: A minimal and carefully ordered layout of color and line in the far corner of the room combines rectilinear green, curved orange, and circular blue.

far right: In another tatami room in the house, an interplay of straight lines and shallow arcs is seen in light shafts on a curved wall.

facing page: The theme of a closing curve from the floor of the room is carried on to the outer entrance's orange sliding door and the frame into which the paper screens slide.

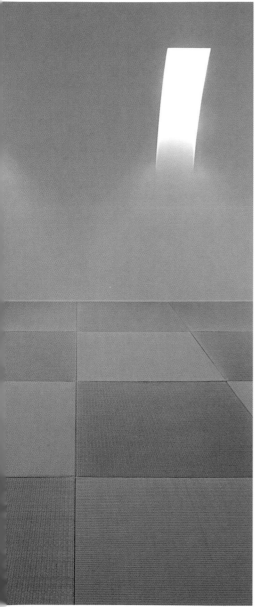

plastic house

One of the visible successes in the work of Kengo Kuma—a star of new Japanese architecture—is his imaginative use of construction materials, looking for the appropriate among unlikely or underutilized sources. For a house in a residential district of Tokyo, designed for a fashion photographer and his writer mother, he chose FRP urethane with an attachment system of plastic screws and plugs. The most plastic part of the Plastic House is the tiny rear garden, with palisades and a raised platform in the surprisingly soft material. Here, Kuma has created a beautifully simple, calm space which, though surrounded by neighboring buildings in this dense area of the city, achieves its intended meditative character through the use of hundreds of regularly spaced plastic slats. Kuma, who says that "if architecture is small and uses humble materials, it can have a good relation with the human body," chose this synthetic material for its soft texture and because "the plastic ages—over time the color changes." And indeed, in the course of visits over two years for this book, the plastic has acquired a gentle green hue. The lightness of the walls and platform comes partly from their changing appearance according to the angle at which they are viewed, while in the evening artificial illumination from the basement well below the platform makes it appear to float.

far right: Viewed from a seated position from one corner of the platform, the space is without decoration. A single tree reflects the soft texture and pale green of the plastic.

right: The parallel arrangement of the plastic slats is concealed when viewed from an angle, as here.

left: In the evening, light from the basement well gives the plastic beams, with their rounded-corner, rectangular cross section, a floating luminosity.

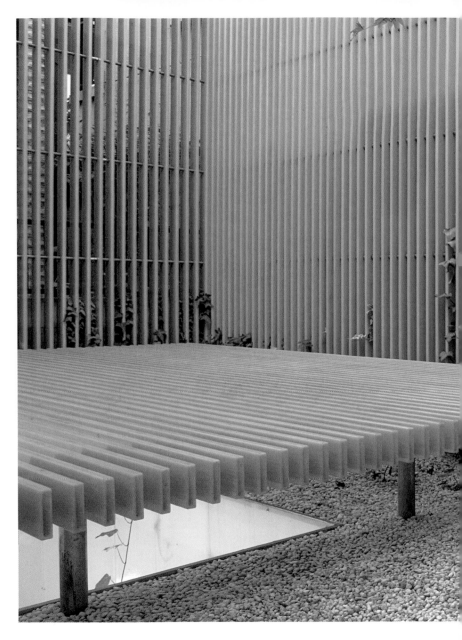

right: A raised platform of beams fills most of the space and is suspended over a basement well that receives daylight during the day and supplies artificial light in the evening.

metal office

The modern need for meditation is increasingly a response to the stress and distraction of the work environment. The habitat that would most benefit from a calm ambience is precisely the one that lacks it. A striking exception is the new offices of the Dynamic Tools Corporation, located in a new academic research town between Kyoto and Osaka and designed specifically to promote a mood of meditation. Award-winning architect Takashi Yamaguchi, whose other commissions include the minimalist Glass Temple and White Temple featured on the following pages, addressed the client's desire to have an environment that was more than just a "box." The office not only had to fit the corporate image of a business carrying out research, development, and the import of precision components, it also had to work as a space that was so simple and inorganic that employees could be freely imaginative in their work.

The entire space is clad in metal (hence the name), including a mixture of .2-inch aluminum laminate and galvanized steel for the exterior and polished aluminum plates for the flooring. To preserve the finish, employees and visitors follow the Japanese domestic tradition of wearing slippers. But Yamaguchi went further than simply executing an all-metal concept: the process of entering the building and walking to the office areas is engineered to create a meditative frame of mind. The entrance hall on the lower floor is filled with light from the floor-to-ceiling frosted glass windows that span the entire frontage. A single, white armchair bathes in this light at the end of a long, narrow hall with polished metal on the facing wall, and the intended mood is bright and serene. What happens next is interesting—polished metal stairs lead up into darkness, lit only by concealed guide lights on

facing page: From the main entrance, a narrow space runs between the glass facade at left and the polished aluminum wall at right to a single white armchair.

either side. At the top, a
return leads through a corridor that is only slightly
less dim, and this opens
out into metallic brightness
once again, in the form of a
spacious meeting room.
On one side of this another
armchair is sited, this time
black. Huge clear glass
windows, each 23 feet
long and 8.5 feet high, are
set on either side, with
translucent blinds that
offer a choice of exposure
to the outside. At .7 inches
thick, the windows block
out exterior noise and pro-

vide a view of a bamboo
grove moving soundlessly
in the wind.

The president's office
adjoins the meeting room,
sided with frosted glass.
Only shadows of the desk
and chair can be seen
mistily from the meeting
room, and a sensitive balance of visibility and privacy ensures that it is not
completely isolated. The
aim is to avoid hierarchical
barriers by unifying this
office and the meeting
room. Inside are only a
desk, chair, computer, and

phone—no papers or any
of the usual office equip-
ment. Yamaguchi's aim in
designing the "Metal
Office" was to "connect
spaces by means of light
and dark, openness and
closure, continuity and dis-
continuity." The entire
building plays its role as a
meditative space.

right: Aluminum steps lead the
visitor from the light of the entrance
into the darkening space above.
facing page: The stairwell as viewed
from the office level. The corridor is
kept dark in preparation for entering
the office area and meeting room.

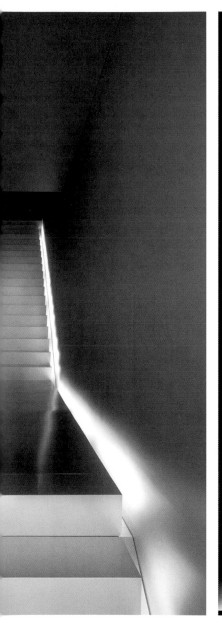

above: The meeting room, in reflecting metal, offers views of the exterior that can be framed with translucent blinds.

facing page: A single black armchair is the counterpart of the white chair in the entrance hall.

facing page: Sandblasted floor-to-ceiling glass walls enclose the president's office on two sides.

above: The interior of the president's office is austerely minimal in both furnishing and tone.

right: With the translucent vertical blinds drawn to the floor, the reflections of soft gray aluminum help to create a space of intentional emptiness.

blue space

American sculptor and designer Danny Lane works principally in glass, which has for him enigmatic and borderline material qualities. "Glass is a supercooled liquid," he says, "and in fact it continues to flow under gravity with imperceptible slowness." It is also, importantly, a material which, at one remove, makes it possible to sculpt with light, and Lane exploits this refractive and reflective control by means of a trademark process of stacking and sculpting hundreds of sheets together. The complex effects from this and from the subtle coloring of glass seen in depth give Lane's monumental works their own internal space. Both of these works, one in Delhi and the other in London, combine this sense of endlessly refracting space with the spatial ambiguity of the empty center. The two parts of each construction change shape and relationship according to where the observer stands, but their facing edges clearly correspond, with the implication of enclosing an emptiness, or nothingness. The awareness of this space in between, whether by words or thought, is a meditation technique. The Delhi piece was named *Shyam* from the Sanskrit term that denotes, in one interpretation at least, the blue space experienced when the mind is on the higher plane of consciousness during meditation and the ego has been transcended. The larger work in London uses low-lead-content glass for a bluer and lighter effect (the lead content in glass gives it its green appearance through selective absorption).

right: Seen in close-up, the individually cut and polished plates of glass refract the setting sun. **far right:** The pale, bright blue color comes from the lower lead content of this glass, which has correspondingly less green in depth.

right: Two twisting stacks of glass stand between two wings of a house in Delhi. One of two works commissioned by Lekha and Ranjan Poddar, the piece is titled *Shyam* for its blue-green internal space and associations with the blue Hindu deity Krishna.

left: In enclosing emptiness,
the two towers of glass in
the London garden, each stacked
in a gently spiraling arrangement,
define a metaphysically
deeper space.

ice chapel

Like glass, ice occupies the transitional zone of materiality, with refraction and the selective absorption of wavelengths creating a near-infinite play of light and color. In addition, it has impermanence, possessing a state which collapses, eventually, into formless water—with all the implications that Buddhist meditation teaches. Each winter, on the banks of the Torne River in Swedish Lapland, a new chapel is designed and constructed in the pure ice for which the river is famous, as part of the Icehotel, an enterprise that has proved remarkably successful in the decade since it began. Each Christmas the chapel is formally handed over to the Jukkasjärvi parish; then in April or May it melts and the water runs back into the river. Although not the first ice chapel (one was built in 1932 on the campus of Lawrence University in Appleton, Wisconsin), it is certainly the best known. Reindeer skins provide insulation from the ice-block pews, and the light filtering through the walls shifts subtly and continuously throughout the short arctic day.

right: Thick round columns of ice lead toward an ice window beyond the altar in a transparent version of the Norman chapel on pages 128–129.

above: From the outside, the chapel and Icehotel take the form of a huge composite igloo embedded in the frozen landscape.

facing page: Reindeer skins, a traditional form of insulation in arctic Scandinavia, cover the ice-block pews.

mid-air

Architect and designer Atsushi Kitagawara deconstructed the traditional Japanese tea-ceremony room to find its metaphysical essentials. "I analyzed the tearoom as form (hardware) and space (software), and I decided to omit all forms, to simply suspend the 'spirits' of the guest and the host in the air." First displayed at the Asia Society in New York in 2002, this ultimate reduction of habitable space is simply the framework of a cube in timber. The forms that Kitagawara refers to are the utensils, the objects for display in the alcove, and the gestures of host and guest as they perform their spiritual exchange. By removing these, he presents a space that requires a thorough contemplation of the process. Only the soul of host and guest exist in the air, and its name, appropriately, is *Chu-ken*, or *Mid-air*. Kitagawara muses that it should be possible to have a tea ceremony purely in the imagination.

facing page: A pure expression of emptiness, yet capable of being filled with the imagination, *Mid-air* is defined by the outline of structure alone.
right: Facing the empty cube is a raised acrylic platform, supported by a steel web, signifying the space for host and guest.

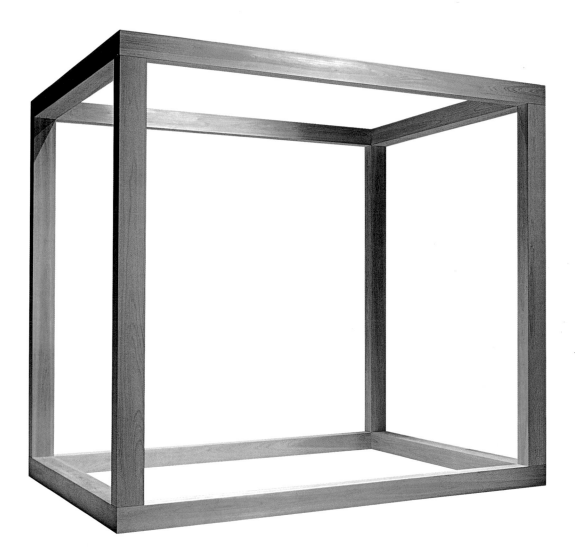

These are meditative spaces that function by altering the immediate environment. Entering them, the user leaves behind the mundane and familiar and steps into a different world, one that brings about a perceptual shift and psychic stimulation.

The idea of changing space implies a relationship with the surroundings, and these spaces have all been built to exist *within* the larger everyday space, whether a room, house, office, or garden. As such, they carry with them sensations of the retreat, haven, and hideaway—what philosopher Gaston Bachelard called "the nooks and corners of solitude." Indeed, the original and primitive space-shift is the corner. As Bachelard continues, "Every corner in a house, every angle in a room, every inch of secluded space in which we like to hide, or withdraw into ourselves, is a symbol of solitude for the imagination; that is to say, it is the germ of a room. . . ."

Most are small, in the spirit of enfolded spaces, and this itself heightens the experience. Rainer Maria Rilke wrote of such places, "And there is almost no space here; and you feel almost calm at the thought that it is impossible for anything very large to hold in this narrowness." Indeed, very little area is needed, because they are all spaces for being still. They ensure immobility. They also ensure a shift in the state of mind. Frenchman Noël Arnaud, in *L'état d'ébauche*, wrote:

Je suis l'espace où je suis

I am the space where I am

house for reading

In her final year in the product design course at the Royal College of Art in London, Yuko Minamide conceived and built a tiny, darkened house which at first appears to have just one purpose—reading without distraction. The thinking behind it goes deeper, as Minamide plays games with scale and the illusion of first appearances. Calling it simply *House/Bed*, she began with the idea of nesting worlds within a world. The pitched-roof house is the icon of Western dwelling, as recognizable on a Monopoly board as in any town built between the nineteenth and twentieth centuries. Minamide took this form, "monolithic when you first see it, and even unfriendly—black with sharp edges," and made a comfortable, isolated, and private space within. The metal frame is clad with black plexiglass, "to assimilate the environment" on the outside and to make the interior seem more spacious. "At first," she says, "people want to keep a distance, but once you get close you can see that it is quite delicate." One end of the frame hinges at the top for access to a room that is essentially a bed fitted with three cushioned holes at the far end, one for the head, the other two for the arms. Beneath, a tray with its own concealed lighting provides the most ergonomically luxurious form for reading, which for Minamide, after the outside space and the black inner space, is the third, interiorized world of the imagination. A small window is cut into one side. "I didn't want the whole thing to become too serious. Instead of reading, you could simply sleep or escape."

facing page: Like a tiny dwelling, *House/Bed* is entered by raising the flap of a wall at one end and climbing inside.

right: A cutaway view shows the
reading position on the black
mattress/floor, with the illuminated
tray slung beneath.
facing page, top: A padded
circular hole cushions the face,
while smaller flanking apertures
fit the arms.
facing page, bottom: *House/Bed*
can also be used for thinking
and relaxation.

Domesticity immediately suggests a kind of bliss, a nest, and a feeling that all is well. But, as with all conditions that are heavily embedded in the human psyche, the reality is more complex, and not necessarily so comforting. English artist Sarah Gillham created an unexpected, burrowing space to explore the deeper meanings of this highly charged aspect of the nurturing home. The form she chose was the sphinx because of the paradox it represents for her in its role as "both protector and destroyer. It guards what is inside but at the same time has the potential for malevolence."

The comfortably lined crawl space is just large enough for one person to enter, and is embedded in a model of the sphinx that is wrapped with that icon of traditional domesticity, a chintz curtain. A flap of this curtain falls to close off the opening, and if there is an element of claustrophobia upon entering, this is entirely consistent with Gillham's purpose, which is to contemplate the way in which enfolding can be both secure and threatening. As Gillham writes, "She holds a space inside of her which is both maternal and sexual. A space to crawl into, to escape, to be consumed and reborn."

facing page: The exterior of the tiny room is modeled on the mythological Sphinx, offspring of the monsters Echidna and Typhon, with the head and upper torso of a woman but the body of a lion.
right: The outer form is given shape by a homely curtain, which adds the sense of the domestic.
far right: One flap of the curtain is lifted at the rear to enter the space, which is comfortably upholstered in white cloth.

curved shoji

For a new family home, architect Michimasa Kawaguchi, who also designed the room in shadows on pages 30–31, had to create independent spaces for the parents and their two sons. This meant three floors above the family business, a body shop for luxury automobiles, and the younger son wanted a space within his apartment that could either open up to all the surrounding modern conveniences or be completely isolated. Kawaguchi accomplished this not only through the physical arrangement of sliding partitions (common in Japan) but also through a total change of style and atmosphere. The result was a semicircular platform that abuts a tiny exterior garden, with sliding paper-clad shoji screens on both sides and a tatami floor. As the varied arrangements on the following pages show, the space can be configured so as to open out onto the garden, or into the living and dining area with its open-plan kitchen. When the sliding screens on both sides are drawn, the "D"-shaped space becomes a world of its own. Kawaguchi's greatest problem was the construction of the curved screens, which of course needed to be handmade. Fortunately, one of the last of the old generation of what we would call cabinetmakers in the West has a workshop nearby and was able to make the frames, albeit with difficulty.

right: An exquisite persimmon bonsai, with miniature autumn fruits, graces the corner of the paper-enclosed space.

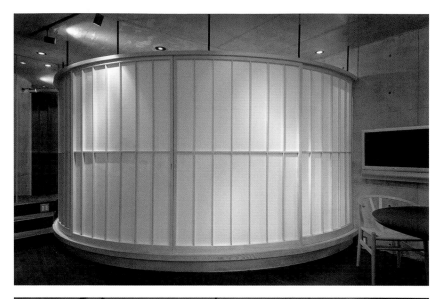

this page and facing page: The paper-clad screens, arranged in the front as an arc and more traditionally flat at the rear, can be configured in many ways to manipulate the space.

above: With the outer, curved screens closed and the flat, inner ones open, the space now relates to the small exterior garden.

facing page: The reverse configuration, with the flat screens shut and the curved ones drawn back, opens the space to the living room and kitchen.

primary colors

Built as a modern version of a tea-ceremony room, but used by its owner as a retreat for an hour or two and for reading quietly, this small circular room is built into a cylindrical tower that rises above one wing of the house. Below is an apartment, with the lower section of the structure containing kitchen fittings. The design is, of course, highly unusual for a Japanese tea-ceremony room, with a primary color scheme in complete contrast to the more usual sub-dued, earthen treatment, and is the creation of architect Kunihiko Hayakawa, whose work frequently has the appearance of stage sets, with compositions reduced to lines, planes, and flat colors. Commissioning circular tatami mats was particularly difficult. A counter-weighted metal ladder can be raised by means of a pulley from the tiny entrance to seal the room off completely.

right: The small cylindrical space has blue walls and a tatami floor, with a red frame around the tiny, elevated entrance.

below left: Seen from the edge of the doorway and flanked by a fixed glass panel and door, the counter-weighted ladder has been raised after entering.

below right: From below, the lowered ladder provides access to the room, which occupies the upper part of the two-story cylinder.

office retreat

Klein Dytham architecture (KDa) has established a strong reputation in Tokyo for innovation and imagination, both of which it brought to the design of the offices for advertising agency Beacon Communications, which occupies four floors of the JR Tokyo Meguro building. The aim was to create an environment that would "promote communication and generate interaction among employees," and attract clients. The first decision was to be

open-plan for all three hundred employees, relatively unusual in hierarchically conscious Japan. Dominating each floor is a huge, flowing slab running the entire floor's length, nearly 200 feet; it undulates and folds to enclose a series of spaces that include meeting rooms, television viewing rooms, a reception area, kitchen, and even a beauty salon. Each floor has its own identity provided by color, materials, and facilities, the four themes being

drawn from the consumer markets that the agency addresses: woman, man, family, and community. The constant interaction and openness is an essential ingredient in the functioning of the agency, but for times when the individual needs to work in privacy, KDa has built into the slab a tiny retreat, accessed by a ladder. This being an advertising agency, however, there is a LAN connection concealed under the pillow!

right: The working environment at Beacon features connected workstations to encourage interaction and the exchange of ideas.

right: A stainless steel ladder leads to a space where a Beacon employee can work without any disruptions or take time out to lie down and think.

ground escape

Shifting space vertically is a clear direction, but one that is not necessarily straightforward to achieve. Both of the previous spaces are elevated, but they take with them sufficient solidity of structure as to create their own new level. Designer Yuko Minamide, who designed the reading house on pages 76–79, saw an alternative habitat in the unused upper volume of interiors, and an escape from the ground level of the rest of the world. Her solution was a ladder with a seat at the top—a 6.5-foot metal-framed chair. "It was also a way of manipulating scale, to create an extraordinary version of an ordinary product," she notes. Despite its size, the chair has a delicate neatness to it, not only because of its small base of 11 square feet, but also by being painted black, giving it a thinner appearance and better definition. The seat is upholstered in leather.

facing page: The structure is part tower, part ladder, and part chair in welded, square-sectioned metal. **right:** For high-ceilinged spaces, the chair inhabits an elevated space that normally is never used.

hut dreams

In the town of Kunitachi, Japan, designer couple Masahisa and Tsuneko Koike took a very ordinary house—a single-story, wooden-frame structure built as cheap housing after the war—and converted the interior into a realization of what Gaston Bachelard calls "the 'hut dream,' which is well-known to everyone who cherishes the legendary images of primitive houses . . . in the house itself a dreamer of refuges dreams of a hut, of a nest, or of a nook and corners in which he would like to hide away." They rendered the interior with a very old technique, in which fine earth is plastered over a framework of woven branches. They used the finely textured silt from rice paddies; to help it adhere with a light coating, they covered the branches with wire netting. Within this hut-like interior, they built two tiny retreats, half hidden under the eaves, providing just enough space for one person to sit quietly in a private world.

The Koikes recently applied this technique, and its connotations of hearth, haven, warmth, and security, to a beauty salon. Salons often are designed to be hip, sharp, and ultramodern, but the idea here was to move away from what is increasingly formulaic. The soft lines and earthen plaster set a more comforting note for the salon's clients.

facing page: A single ladder serves both tiny perchlike spaces, as Bachelard says, ". . . at the house's center, in the circle of light shed by the lamp. . . ."
right: The fine silt, bonding to the framework of branches and wire netting, crazes as it dries into a natural pattern.
page 96: The second earth-clad perch is slightly higher than the first, reached with some agility from the ladder.
page 97: The same concept and wall surface was used professionally by the designers to impart a relaxing atmosphere to a beauty salon.

room on a perch

In a small temple hidden in the heart of downtown Kyoto, Hitoshi Akino, a priest, and his wife included a backyard with no purpose other than to house the toilet. This was destroyed in the Kobe earthquake of 1995, after which a modern flush toilet was built inside. This left Akino with a derelict space that he was sure could be put to better use, and he contacted architect Terunobu Fujimori to devise a kind of tea-ceremony room. "Kind of"

because Fujimori, who is a professor of architectural history at Tokyo University, takes a distinctly quirky, almost Bohemian, approach to design. His idea was to create something like a stubby tree house, perched in one corner to look back toward the temple. First he found a chestnut tree with a suitable three-pronged fork in the communal forest by his hometown in Chino. This was cut, moved to Kyoto, and embedded in a concrete base in the corner. Most of the con-

struction, including the leaded window and sheet-copper roofing, was in fact done by Akino, supervised by Fujimori during visits to the site every two or three months. Although the floor area is tiny—only 39 square feet—the oversize window, which slides into the wall, and the white plastered interior walls give it a relatively spacious feeling. Entry is another matter. Even by the standards of tea-ceremony rooms, which have a purposefully

low entrance (called the "wriggling-in entrance"), the tiny trapdoor at the top of a wooden ladder is a tight squeeze. Akino and Fujimori joke that it seems more like "an opening for removing night soil (human waste that collects in outside toilets)."

facing page: Seen from the living room, the small garden with the perched room is in the far corner.

facing page: The yard has been turned into a garden of white river gravel, across which stepping stones meander from the living room, under a grassy arch (an homage to Le Corbusier) and past an undulating grassy pipe (a nod to Salvador Dalí's soft objects).

left: The interior is furnished with simple leather cushions. Instead of a traditional scroll on the wall, Akino placed the last drawing made by his mother, a well-known painter.

below: The leaded windows provide a view onto the garden and living quarters of the temple.

left: Over, rather than under, a spreading chestnut tree, the room has the appearance of an elves' dwelling from mythology. Access is via the short ladder underneath.

the peace of transience

A new garden to face a guesthouse at Gion-ji temple in Mito, Ibaragi Prefecture, was designed by Shunmyo Masuno to create an atmosphere of peace and calm. Called *Shofu-tei*, Pine Maple Garden, it combines maple trees with the Japanese black pines that have been in the temple grounds for as long as anyone can remember. Seen from the raised floor of the guesthouse, which in traditional Japanese fashion is fronted with sliding screens, the flowing horizontal arrangement of moss, white gravel, stones, and low trees promotes tranquility. It also offers food for contemplation on the transience of nature, yet an acceptance of change, to be identified with one's own life. A wall separates this garden from another, featured on pages 140–141, with a more focused, energetic theme, that of endeavor. A raised wooden walkway connects the two different spaces.

right: The pattern of raked gravel is an integral part of the design of dry-stone gardens, and it is carefully preserved year after year.
below: Replanted pines and newly planted maples inhabit islands of moss in a braided river of gravel. Behind the wall lies another Masuno garden, depicting the parable of the carp at the Dragon Gate.

childhood memories

Anne Wood, television producer and creator of many children's programs, including the hugely successful *Teletubbies*™, bought the land for her new house in the west of England largely on the strength of the brook and willow trees at the end of the plot. It reminded her of walks along the banks of another stream that she took as a child, and she wanted to recapture that sense. About a hundred yards from the house, this private spot was to be her "getaway place," and she wanted a structure that would be its focus. "I don't want to use clichés such as 'finding the inner child,' but in what I do it's important somehow to keep a link with childhood." Interior designer and architect Charles Rutherford recommended artist Rosie Leventon as someone who could capture the spirit of the place, and after consultations she created this structure in steel and chain link. For Wood, it had "all kinds of resonances," including vernacular architecture, a "slight eighteenth century feel," and symbolism of spring—"like a snowdrop, but larger." There is a curious asymmetry to the profile that takes time to grasp, and becomes apparent only when one walks around the stream and garden, while the odd combination of substantial steel construction and transparency is designed to invoke reflections on one of the fundamentals of childhood—the safety of an enfolding space.

right: Seen from the house, the silvery structure aligns with the long rectangular pond, which is flanked on one side by wildflowers and on the other by a lawn.

right: The stream at the end of the garden, with its grasses and overhanging willow, is the setting for the asymmetrical, peaked structure.

following pages: The interior reveals curved steel ribs and a simple arched entrance. Steel and chain link stretched taut on the tubular steel frame form gently curved walls.

briefcase room

A designer and professor at the Tohoku University of Art and Design, Toshihiko Suzuki maintains a fascination with aluminum, which is for him "the best material with which to create a balance between furniture and architecture." He is also concerned with the dichotomy between traditional Japanese tatami culture and the modern, and has brought both together in this unique portable meditative space: a mobile tatami room that unfolds from a slim, if slightly oversize, brief-case. The exterior is of .4-inch-thick aluminum honeycomb panels, engi-neered to contain a three-quarter-size tradi-tional tatami in *igusa* straw and a retractable table. Shelter, of a deliberately conceptual kind, is provided by white sail-like panels attached to a tensioned structure of alu-minum poles and rubber shock cords that follows the geodesic designs of Buckminster Fuller. Suzuki's intention was a personal space that contains an icon of tradi-tional culture embedded in metal, capable of being erected anywhere.

right: The erected space, with a superstructure of aluminum poles and shock cords, as viewed against the designer's countryside atelier.
below: When closed, the entire structure, with a three-quarter-size tatami mat and folding table, folds neatly into the 5-inch-thick case.

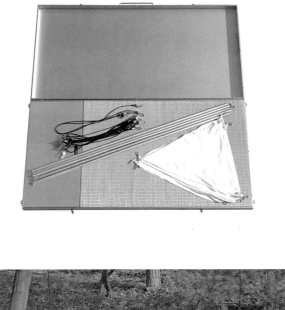

these pages, left to right: Sail-like triangles of cloth attach to the tensioned framework of poles for partial shelter, with the lid partly raised as a wall.

right: The designer calls the
structure, here set up in
the woods, Ichijyo, meaning
"one full tatami size."

falling spheres

Artist Yukako Shibata draws her inspiration from the fugitive colors of the natural world: "Elements like water, atmosphere, snow, and bubbles exist for us through the complex interplay of light, local environment, and the human perceptual system. In this cylindrical space, just enough for one person to stand inside, I wanted to create the experience of the ephemeral." Using hundreds of lightweight, hand-sculpted spheres dipped in plaster and painted in soft colors, she created a shifting curtain that surrounds and encloses the person inside. "The idea originated from snow falling when you look up to the sky—the flakes fall everywhere equally, but for each person they appear to fall only toward you. What we look at is not always what exists. We each create our own world of perception."

The spheres are hung from a hoop using thin nylon line in a way that allows them to interact individually and in groups as they move. She chose spheres as a universal but abstract form, and employed her own subtle techniques of coloring to make a "physical version of light and water and the evanescence of bubbles." It was important to allow the imperfections of accident in creating each sphere to give them individual, organic forms. The expansion of the foam core from which each one grew was different every time, as was the application of plaster and pigment. "Both the process and the purpose are linked. Making is a form of meditation for me, and the space itself is for meditation," she explains.

facing page: Suspended from a metal hoop, the 6.5-foot-tall circular curtain of spheres hangs clear of the ground, and is entered by ducking under the lower edge to stand inside.
right: The process of dipping the carved, expanded foam in plaster, and the plaster's interaction with the varied texture of the foam, give each sphere a fragile, organic individuality that is enhanced by its subtle coloring.

the persistence of red

Overlapping paper banners in a range of powerful, intense reds are suspended from floor to ceiling to transform an interior into a mesmerizing and fragile space. The arrangement of these gently moving walls by artist Chris Cook is site-specific, creating a unique environment each time. Cook draws heavily on her Chinese cultural heritage, and the colors are based on her memories of places, events, and objects from her childhood in East Asia, in particular "the smell of burning incense, the dimness of temple interiors, the sacred environment filled with noises and the ever-present color of red, forming a continuous background to ceremony and prayers, social and spiritual connections." She takes large-scale paper monochrome banners and paints them with layers of acrylic to create a specific hue, shade, and density for each one. By overlapping them in depth and allowing the lightweight paper to float and move, she makes an architectural space that, while ephemeral, manages to close off the outside environment completely. The modulation of reds—some hotter and advancing, others cooler and receding—adds to the three-dimensional effect. As Cook writes, "The physical presence is created to overwhelm and to create an atmosphere of silence and contemplation."

below: A panoramic view of the installation in a London studio, with a counter laid out with samples.
following pages: The overlapping of the individually painted sheets of paper, each a slightly different color, extends the viewer's attunement to the spatial dimension of red.

right: The lightness and gentle
movement of the hanging sheets
has the contradictory effect
of expanding the sense of space.

samye

Soft enclosures, such as those explored by Yukako Shibata and Chris Cook on the previous pages, have a curiously endless quality. A wall is a wall, with solidity and definition. It encloses Cartesian space. Soft and moving boundaries, however, mark no definite limits and hint at infinity. One of the oldest extant meditative spaces in Buddhism is the *dukhang*, or assembly hall, at the Tibetan monastery of Samye in Dranang, where huge cloth banners line the walls and rows of pillars to create a dreamlike world of dim, incense-impregnated space. They also help to invert the normal play of natural light in an interior. The only daylight that filters through small windows set high along one wall is caught by the tops of the banners. This is where Buddhism first reached Tibet, in AD 779, when the monastery was founded by Padmasambhava. Although damaged by earthquake, fire, and the Chinese Cultural Revolution, Samye endures. Prayer and meditation have filled this space for centuries.

far right: Cloth banners, some brocaded and others dyed, mask the solid surfaces of pillars and walls in Samye's *dukhang*.
right: Student monks meditate beneath the tall banners at one end of the hall.

Contemplation can be generalized and, as we saw in the classic *zazen* form of meditation in the first chapter, the immediate goal may be to empty the mind of thought—to "think what you do not think," in the words of a Zen master. But it may also have a specific purpose, a focus. This comes in two forms. One is a particular topic or theme that the space presents to the person entering, and the exemplar of this is a certain kind of Zen garden that is representational. Those shown here are all modern. The second form is preparation for a specific activity or event, such as in the arts: painting, sculpting, writing, dancing. Then there is mortality itself, for which there are spaces designed to help in the planning of the passing of life.

Of course, even though it uses the technique of "nonthinking," *zazen* is highly focused—on the ultimate goal of enlightenment—but for many this is a lofty ideal, and these seemingly more practical ends are easier to achieve. Focus is also apparent in a more obvious way: in the design of a space that visually directs the eye and gives it, and the mind, something to hold onto—a tangible motif or icon.

vigil

Two rows of massive round piers support unmolded arches under a tunnel-vaulted nave, all in stone imported from France, to create the Chapel of St. John the Evangelist in the Tower of London, originally built as William the Conqueror's great fortress by the Thames. It hardly seems possible that this monumental construction, austere but luminous, could be an upper-floor room, but it is indeed embedded within the eleventh-century White Tower. This was where medieval knights of the Order of the Bath, the second highest order of chivalry in England, spent a night of prayer and meditation before receiving knighthood. The vigil, as well as the ritual purification that gave the order its title, was abandoned in the nineteenth century, but up until that time the knight knelt before the altar, facing south, until the morning light flooded the undecorated stone hall, as it does here.

facing page: Daylight floods the altar and nave, marking the end of the night's vigil.

Although meditation is inextricably associated with Zen, Theravada Buddhism, which is the more traditional and conservative branch of the doctrine and is followed in Southeast Asia, also teaches it as a means of attaining enlightenment. Indeed, Theravada's ascetism and strict insistence on finding one's own path through observance and meditation set it apart from Mahayana Buddhism, the "Great Vehicle," which made the doctrine compatible with everyday life and is practiced eastward from Tibet. The greatest of all Buddhist cities, nevertheless, was Pagan (today known as Bagan), built on the banks of the Irrawaddy River in Burma (Myanmar); at its height, from the middle of the eleventh century to the end of the thirteenth, it had some 13,000 religious buildings, spread across the plain as far as the eye could see. The more than 2,000 surviving temples, monasteries, and chapels, mostly in brick, contain a multitude of quiet, darkened spaces for meditation.

facing page: A statue of the Buddha at Dhammayangyi temple, in Pagan, sitting in *bhumisparsa mudra*, the posture signifying the complete conquest of ignorance. Each of the several mudras helps to focus the mind in a different way.
right: A tiny chapel at Shwezigon pagoda, with a kneeling statue of the Buddha's disciple Ananda.

a priest's garden

Another, but very private, space at Gion-ji temple (see pages 10–13, 104–105 and 140–141) is the small walled garden of the chief priest. Against the empty backdrop of white walls and framed on the left and right by stands of bamboo, a single upright stone dominates the composition and holds the attention, the more so when spotlit in the evening. At the stone's base a bed of white gravel flows between mounds of moss to lap at the priest's study, representative not just of a river but of the flow of history in this 350-year-old temple. The present incumbent is the twenty-sixth in a line of responsibility handed down from generation to generation, and the garden is designed for contemplation of this. History flows, things change, and this temple has been active in communicating Zen through redesigning its buildings and gardens. The core, however, remains constant, as the rock continues to remind.

right: A white wall fills the framed view from the study, providing an infinite background to the carefully focused scene that centers on the upright stone.

Zen gardens, several of which are featured in this book, are above all functional, designed specifically for meditation. The theme may be difficult for the untrained to discern, as in Ryoan-ji (pages 40–41), but there is always a purpose. Above all, Zen gardens are focused. In *Reading Zen in the Rocks*, professor of Japanese art and history François Berthier writes, "In the realm of art [Zen monks] privileged the garden most of all as a means of expres-

sion." Shunmyo Masuno, who created this work here, explains that "you have to go straight to the heart of the matter and create something which will have a lasting impression on people." Masuno, as the premier exponent of modern Zen gardens, wants to make the means for self-discovery and meditation available to everyone. In this garden-for-viewing at the center of a hotel in central Tokyo, he has symbolized the Buddhist universe with three groupings of

eleven rocks into five, three, and three. Three rocks represent the three worlds of Buddhism, and the central group of five rocks, on a mossy mound, represents the five peaks of the cosmic mountain Sumeru (Shumi-sen) at the center of the universe. The sun and moon revolve around Sumeru, and here a circle chiseled into the face of one rock represents the former, while a crescent on a rock on the other side of the mound symbolizes the moon.

far right: Seen from the side, the central grouping of rocks includes one, at right, from which issues a river of white gravel, with a crescent moon carved into its face.
right: The main viewing place for the enclosed garden is a tatami room. The carved circle representing the sun is on the stone nearest the window.

Another meditation garden by Masuno fills the space at the rear of Rensho-ji temple, near Yokohama, and is called Fusho-tei, or Spiritual Beacon. The theme is that there is always a constant, even during times of rapid change. For Zen this constant is "truth" or "teachings," for which the founder of this temple, the fourteenth-century monk Rensho, was famous. Masuno explains: "There is a Zen word *whoabaa* which means that even on a rapidly flowing river the moon shadow on the water's surface holds steady and still. There are many people flowing by on the swift currents of the world. As they are unable to discover their own moon shadow, they become water. The theme of this garden is to rekindle our predecessor's teachings." A river of stones issues from a waterfall and flows through the garden, under a bridge and toward the reception hall, from where it can be viewed. A standing stone represents Rensho the teacher, to oversee and guide people into the future.

facing page: From a hidden source higher up the slope among the trees, the flow of rocks debouches at the feet of the viewer seated in the open-sided hall.
right: At a higher point, the dry-stone river flows under a natural bridge and around a large rock.

right: To the right of the river of
stones, where it laps at the edge of
the raised flooring, stand a granite
well and water basin.

morality tale

This is probably the most narrative and representational of Shunmyo Masuno's modern Zen gardens. It is intended for individual meditation, with a square seat of stone placed, very unusually, *within* the sea of white gravel (Zen gardens are almost universally for *looking at*). The setting is the quiet, provincial temple of Gion-ji in Mito, Ibaragi Prefecture, and the scene laid out in stone is a metaphor for endeavor couched in a historical event from the seventeenth

century. In Zen, the aim is to elevate oneself to new heights step by step through ascetic training, and the waterfall is seen as a hurdle to break through— and so reach new ground.

A well-known Chinese fable tells of a waterfall known as the Dragon Gate, plunging "more swiftly than an arrow shot by a strong archer." In the basin below it, hundreds of carp gather, hoping to climb the falls, for any which succeed will be transformed into a dragon. Buddhist priests

have long used this tale to illustrate the endurance and ambition needed to attain enlightenment, and in the seventeenth century in Mito, the enlightened feudal ruler Tokugawa Mitsukuni invited a learned monk from Nagasaki called Shin-etsu to teach. In this stone tableau, the largest of the upright stones on the left is the priest, and the pyramidal stone at the back Mitsukuni; the Dragon Gate is at the back on the right, faced by the small stone—the carp— in the pool of white stones.

right: A square hewn stone has been placed as a meditation seat in the center of this modern Zen garden. Under the plum tree at left, upright stones represent an audience that includes the vice-shogun listening to a priest explaining the meaning of the parable of the carp at the Dragon Gate, seen at right beyond the stone bridge.

a sculptor's room

Aji on the southern Japanese island of Shikoku is a stonemasons' town, at the foot of a granite mountain that has been quarried for centuries, and it was here where the famous Japanese-American sculptor Isamu Noguchi eventually worked, lived, and is buried. Masatochi Izumi, who was born into a family of stone carvers, was Noguchi's principal collaborator for twenty-two years until the latter's death, and with the team of artisans he assembled to work on the monumental sculptures has completed some of the best-known architectural stone projects in Japan, in addition to his own sculpting. In a world dominated by the creative and spiritual potential of stone, Izumi created for himself a hand-built house of granite, adjoining his mason's yard. Within it, one room was created for quiet contemplation— sliding shoji screens on two sides flank a massive wall that Izumi assembled from granite stones of different sizes. The paper of the sliding screens and the open steel trusses of the roof contrast with the solidity of the stone. Outside this room, Izumi built a circular freestanding granite structure, its round interior dimly lit with low windows, for studying and for entertaining friends.

right: The massive wall is a very personal creation, an assembly over time of carefully chosen stones, their natural outlines preserved by using a range of sizes to fit.

above: In a small courtyard that separates the room on the previous pages from the rest of the house, Izumi built a circular, independent stone room.

above: A low round table with
simply cut logs for seats echoes the
circular space, which receives
its subdued illumination through
small, low windows.

qi in a miniature landscape

Chitoshi Kihara and Yasujirou Aoki, who created the room looking out onto a pebble pond on pages 38–39, here worked on another small garden space overlooked by a tatami room that projects out above it. With the sliding screen open, it presents a detailed scene for contemplation. In this case, the pond and rocks are more representational, and the entire design, from the configuration of the space to the plantings, is focused on directing the flow of energy (qi) outward from the corner. This narrowing of the space was unavoidable because of the shape of the plot, but Kihara installed a curved, rendered wall. Aoki designed a pond with a base of black pebbles set in concrete, from which emerge a slope of larger pebbles leading to rocks and plantings—ocean, beach, and forested mountains. A camellia and blue oak face back to diffuse the negative energy in the corner, while a maple faces outward to help direct the positive flow of energy.

far right: A chromed-steel pillar, supporting the projecting roof of the small room, reflects the pool, stones, and trees of the small landscape.
right: The curving wall and expanding body of water channel the energy flow outward from the corner.

alcove

The alcove, or tokonoma, in a traditionally configured Japanese room is both a place for the display of a seasonal object and a point of focus in an otherwise spare interior. As with the modern redesign of the tea-ceremony room, this alcove too has been subject to different interpretations. It originally included a hanging scroll and a container with a flower (or something approaching it, like a twig). Tenshin Okakura in *The Book of Tea* stresses the impor-

tance of visual focus in a meditative space: "Just as one cannot listen to different pieces of music at the same time, a real comprehension of the beautiful being is possible only through concentration upon some central motive." Here and on the following pages are modern expressions of this device to focus attention. Inevitably, the form of a recess suggests the formation of a different kind of space. Traditional tokonoma were unlit; as Junichiro Tanizaki

observed, "An empty space is marked off with plain wood and plain walls, so that the light drawn into it forms dim shadows within emptiness. There is nothing more." Modern alcoves often reverse this lighting dynamic so that they appear either as a source of light or as an opening into light.

far right: A modern tea-ceremony room by designer Yukio Hashimoto for his own house, with the alcove placed at one side. The asymmetric layout is enhanced by the split-level ceiling, concealed lighting, and the differently shaped tatami mats.
right: Hashimoto's alcove has a rough, earthen render to the wall and a red-lacquered lower surface, on which is displayed a simple flower arrangement in a gray, half-moon vase.

above: In the Tofu House, so-called for its massive, white cubic form, architect Jun Tamaki combined an asymmetrically shaped alcove with a window.

facing page: At the entrance to the paper-enclosed meditative space featured on pages 14–21, Tetsuo Goto installed an alcove with concealed overhead lighting and a granite shelf supported by a rough stone wall.

above: In two different commissions, Goto replaced the idea of a vase for flower displays with a shallow, water-filled depression. Here, the circular indentation is carved into a granite slab.

facing page: In this example, the depression is in red-lacquered wood, its polished surface reflecting daylight through a tall, narrow window that replaces a hanging scroll.

A form of alcove is the central focus of Shunmyo Masuno's design for Opus Arisugawa, a luxury condominium completed in 2004. Close to Roppongi Hills in Minami-Azabu, the building is in the center of Tokyo, and Masuno decided to adapt some of the principles used in the approach to temple design, so as to progressively diminish the noise and chaos of the city. Typically, a temple (and other sanctuaries) can be entered from different directions through the gates known as San-mon. These, and the paths that lead to them, act to purify the soul in the transition from the profane to the sacred. At the condominium, Masuno uses two sinuous lines of differently sourced and configured stones to penetrate the building from the street and from the rear courtyard. At the beginning, an assembly of massive granite walls—white, roughly chiseled stone framed by polished black—curves inward to lead the way. This becomes a single wall with flowing water to begin muffling the street noise, and then a diminishing line of stone that cuts through the glass wall of the entrance to come to rest at a large alcove that is the focal point for the lobby. Another lower line of stone snakes through the rear courtyard to cut through a glass window, also into the lobby.

far right: The focal point is a greatly enlarged version of a tokonoma, or alcove, facing and just inside the entrance. Concealed lighting behind the curved wall helps both to project it forward and provide contrast. A single, unadorned white vase on a polished black stone shelf occupies the focal point.
right: The wall is covered with crumpled sheets of handmade Japanese paper, stained with persimmon tannin.
center: A pattern of rough chiseling on the granite plinth contrasts with the coarse texture of the rendering on the surrounding wall.

above: Curving in parallel, a group of walls marks the start of the stonework at street level.
right: High polish and rough chiseling create textural contrast in the stone surfaces to engage attention.

right: The stone pathway from the rear courtyard divides into two—rough and polished—and penetrates the glass window.

painter's stone

The painter Akira Kaho (winner of the Japan Art Prize) sited his studio at the top of a bi-level garden in Kyoto. The garden itself was created by garden designer Atsushi Akenuki as a way for Kaho to prepare for painting as he walked up the path from the house. The prime meditative focus, however, was reserved for the space immediately in front of the studio. In the tradition of obsession with a particular rock, which goes back to at least the sixteenth century and the purchase of the famous Fujito Rock, Kaho had had his eye on one special stone for two decades before he could afford to buy it at a staggering cost of twenty million yen (190,000 U.S. dollars). Called a *sajiishi*, it is unique, with a flat top eroded into a complex of deep runnels, as if some strange worms had tunneled into it. When the painter in his studio slides back the screen door, the entrance frames this spectacular natural form.

right: Seen from the transom of the studio, rainwater courses through the runnels that craze the surface of the black stone.

dancer's shrine

In Bali's rich cultural life, dance fulfills a number of functions that go deeper than theatrical perform-ance. The many forms of Balinese dance are chiefly directed toward the gods, for propitiation, gratitude, entertainment, and as a channel between the divine and the material world. With more than a thousand troupes on the island, dance is vital and permeates village life. Before a performance, dancers attend their spe-cific local shrine for *taksu*, or inspiration, from the gods. Close to Sanur in the south of the island, between the villages of Semawang and Intaram, is the dancers' shrine of Pura Dalem Sembawa. The top of the shrine is decorated with a representation of a dancer's headdress.

far right: The tiny dancers' shrine is squeezed between two others in the temple complex.
right: The shrine is capped with the form of a Balinese dancer's headdress.
center: One of the two sculpted guardian deities flanking the base of the shrine.

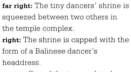

meditation wall

Writer, art director, and longtime Bali resident Leonard Lueras designed this partly open area for meditation on the ground floor of his house in Taman Mertasari, using the four essential themes that pervade the island's life: dance, painting, water, and Balinese Hinduism. The broad entrance area that separates the two wings of the house is open at the back, and here Lueras built a small pond from which rises a wall with this bas-relief. The corner angle of floor tiles provides space for seated meditation, and the bas-relief, the icon for focus and concentration. This represents the Hindu concept of Triloka, or "three worlds," with the supreme Balinese deity Sanghyang Widhi dancing on the world mountain, symbolically appearing in phallic form. Lueras had the design created in Kamasan village, famed for its traditional painting that follows precise iconographic rules, in which the outlines are first drawn in black ink. This was then cast into paras, blocks of volcanic pumice cement.

far right: Floor tiles project into the pond at the base of the wall and create a space for sitting.
right: The deity Sanghyang Widhi dancing on a stylized and phallic representation of the world mountain.

generations

An unusual project for artist and garden designer Takeshi Nagasaki involved creating a topographically precise and functional space for a cemetery. The task had been left to the client by his father, and on the death of the latter a space was set aside in the temple grounds, but at a distance from the other family tombs. It was Nagasaki's sense of spatial organization that brought him the commission, which involved an arrangement of sculptures repre-

right: The space is defined by bronze monoliths representing the father and his wife (in the center) and two sons, with the urn set in the floor in the middle.

senting the family. Nagasaki first chose a natural stone with the dimensions of the father, and from this carved three sculptures, each with an incised niche to give them a directional shape. These were then cast in bronze, and that of the father and his wife were sited to face the ancestor's tombs, which meant a 45-degree angle to the plot. The other two, each representing a son, face toward it. Between them is the embedded urn, intended to be walked on

by anyone entering the space. This was covered with a bronze lid cast from branches of a persimmon tree and bamboo, both of which the father loved.

166 **oratorio**

An oratory is a small chapel or room built for private worship. This, the oratorio of Peñas Negras, near Taos, New Mexico, adjoins the cemetery, or *camposanto*, where it has been used for at least a century and a half by women of the community to keep vigil while the men dig the grave of the deceased. The serene simplicity of the interior, its mud-plastering interrupted only by a single niche carved out of adobe to hold the crucifix and candles, accords with its quiet function as a space for remembrance. According to adobe historian Orlando Romero, "This meditative space is a reminder of the times when priests were few and far between, and religious practice was left up to the Hispanic villagers themselves."

facing page: The sole focus and decoration of the oratory's interior is a shallow niche in the adobe wall.
right: The exterior of the simple adobe building, opens to the full width of the facade.

contemplating mortality

In the crematorium at Hofu in the far south of Japan, Shunmyo Masuno, whose Zen garden constructions we saw on pages 134–141, has created a contemplative spiritual garden to assist the families of the deceased. As Masuno explains, "No living being remains in the present world forever. It is the unchangeable rule of the natural world. The great leaders of religion, land, and man have not been able to escape death." In this space, seen by mourn-

ers immediately after a cremation, he created a metaphor for the acceptance of mortality by symbolizing the forty-nine-day process of becoming Buddha after death. In Mahayana Buddhism, this is the period of transitional state once all the stages of death have occurred and before the next life—the time it takes for the dissolution of consciousness. According to belief, Siddhartha Gautama achieved Buddhahood during his lifetime in the

course of forty-nine days seated under a tree. The circular basin is in polished black granite, filled with water to represent the sky—*kuu*. The rippling reflections of the scenery represent the uncertainty of material existence. A progression of six arcs of the same polished black granite around the pool represent the first six weeks, and the final week, the attainment of Buddhahood, is symbolized by the raw granite boulder emerging from the water.

far right: The large main garden at the entrance symbolizes aspects of the departure from life. The inorganic area at the back represents the afterlife with its distant mountains, the lush organic space in the foreground represents the world, and the flowing white sand the River Styx.
right: Seen from above, the circular granite pond of the garden at the rear represents the transition from this world to the next.
following pages: Arcs of cut stone revolve around the black basin to culminate in a granite boulder that seems to climb out of the water. The cremation chamber is at the right, behind the low window.

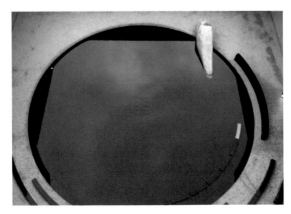

At the beginning, I mentioned Martin Heidegger's argument that establishing a location is the first act necessary in order to allow for a space to be created. But location can also be a source, or conduit, of power. The (much trivialized in the West) feng shui is a Chinese practice to ensure that the places where we dwell are built and arranged in harmony with qi, the flow of energy that animates human beings and has its source in the single "breath at the origin of things, forever circulating" (Guo Pu writing in the fourth century). According to this widely held belief, certain locations and orientations allow one to tap into the energy of the world more easily. Less mystically, the genius loci is the specificity of a site, and if we take an existential view of place and space, locations have meaning. Awareness of the unique character of a place—not necessarily because of a spiritually conceived energy such as qi, but through memory or the accumulation of historical associations—can bring power to the mind. More than this, a meditative space can gather energy through its geometry, of which the pyramid in Western thought and the pagoda in the East are enduring forms.

Stones, as we've seen, have had spiritual significance across history, culture, and faith. In Hindu cults, particularly Saivite, "naturally occurring" stones—*svayambhu*—are rare and of special importance. Their particular significance is that they represent, without human intervention, the god Shiva in his essential form as the lingam. To the Khmers, who built the sanctuary (at right) around one such earthborn image of Shiva, the powerful natural energy of the site was without question. And all the more so because it was not far from another famous svayambhu, the huge rock on top of the mountain above Wat Phu in Laos. The sanctuary here, Ta Muen Thom, is on the very edge of the Dongrek escarpment, the border between Thailand and Cambodia. Building the substantial temple, which took place in the eleventh century, involved extending out over the escarpment in order to keep the stone at its center.

At the heart of the ancient Khmer empire, in Angkor, major temples drew their strength from being constructed as microcosms of the universe, thus ensuring a direct connection to its center. This, as we saw in the Zen garden on pages 134–135, was Mount Sumeru with its five peaks and a central summit surrounded by four smaller ones. With minor variations, this cosmology was shared by Hinduism and Buddhism. Centuries later, and long after most of the temples were abandoned, Theravadan Buddhists use the most intimate of the stone shrines and spaces for prayer and meditation, believing the carved stones to hold power.

facing page: This stone and its pedestal were discovered in situ at some time in the eleventh century on the edge of the plateau that now separates Cambodia from Thailand. Its natural power as a lingam was considered so significant that the entire temple of Ta Muen Thom was built around it.

above: One of the many enigmatic, giant carved faces at the long-abandoned temple of Bayon in Angkor looks on as an elderly Khmer woman in a tiny stone room kneels in front of a salvaged statue of the Buddha.

facing page: In the nearby twelfth temple of Preah Khan, local Buddhists found a bas-relief of a female divinity half buried in a collapsed gallery, and now regard it as a source of power.

notre-dame

The top-floor apartment of photographer Bernard Hermann overlooks not just one of the world's most famous sights, the cathedral of Notre-Dame de Paris, but also the historical and official heart of the city—*"Kilomètre Zero."* This is the reference point for all distances along highways starting in Paris, and it predates the French city. Before the cathedral, which was built between 1163 and 1345, there stood Paris's first Christian church, the Basilica of Saint Etienne, and before this there was a Roman temple to Jupiter, standing just inside the main gates to what was a Roman city. All of this imbues the spot with a particular significance, and for many years Hermann has built up a remarkable series of images of *"Kilomètre Zero,"* being published in a book of the same name. For his meditation practice, he determined to build a space that would tap into this special location. He bought what was originally a small attic with roof access, and extended the access steps that originally led down to the communal stairwell so that they would enter the apartment. The room is tiny, but with a window that frames a unique view of Notre-Dame. Hermann raised the level so that the cathedral would be visible from a seated meditation position, adding a long mirror on the opposite wall for a second view. A tree took root on the ledge just outside from a seed blown by the wind or carried by a bird, gradually building its presence.

right: The only object of significance is a Tibetan tanka representing Amitayus, the Buddha of Infinite Light. For Hermann this acts as a "rosary"— an object to hold in the mind and on which to focus.

following pages: The twin towers of Notre-Dame, framed perfectly in the window, are reflected in a mirror running the length of the opposite wall.

the tree

The tree, as a symbol of growth, nurturing, and stability, has been a locus of strength in many cultures, as witness the widespread mythology of the tree of life. In Bodh Gaya, India, one species—the pipal or *Ficus religiosa*—has extra significance as the place of shelter where Siddhartha Gautama achieved nirvana through seven weeks of meditation, becoming Buddha. As a result, the species is known throughout the East as the *bodhi* tree—the tree of enlighten- ment. The saffron-wrapped tree that now spreads its branches over Buddhists who come from all over the world is a descendant of the original. If we think of the Shinto practice of constant rebuilding to keep the constant (pages 232–233), the tree that now defines the ultimate meditation space combines both origin (genetically) and original form (for Gautama it would have appeared like this).

below: Wrapped in the saffron cloth used for monks' robes, the *bodhi* tree at Bodh Gaya, next to the Mahabodhi Temple, is the place where the Master achieved enlightenment—the ultimate goal of Buddhism.

right: Near the *bodhi* tree at Bodh Gaya, Tibetan monks on pilgrimage to India prostrate themselves under the spreading branches of another, similar tree.

When ceramic artist Yuuichi Kurosawa moved back to the wooded mountains of his native Chichibu, he wanted a "serene space" where he could contemplate before working, and sought inspiration in the grove of cherry trees in front of the house (which he and his wife completed with recycled railway sleepers). He felt a "natural energy" in these trees that he could draw upon. The structure that translated this initial notion into reality was the result of a workshop project directed by architect Takuto Hiki for his students at Meiji University. The team decided on the metaphysical roundness of an egg as the theme, to be rendered in mostly natural materials from the locality. The plan is circular, with the entrance facing due south, on a raised stone foundation. Recycled timber—such as that from old railway sleepers of Aomori cedar—were used as much as possible for the structure, including the circular walls, plastered with local clay, and the saddle roof. Inside, a raised mortar plinth, also circular, supports twelve cypress poles arranged in a circle and enclosing an elevated wooden floor. A succession of triangular windows around the circumference allows sunlight to enter throughout the day, and the twelve timbers act as a sundial. Charcoal was placed under the wooden floor both to absorb moisture and to generate negative ions. In its location, materials, and communal building, the tiny space is perfectly made for woodland contemplation.

facing page: Seen from the entrance, a raised circular platform of wood sits on a plinth of mortar, surrounded by twelve posts of cypress.
right: The planks from which the platform is constructed are recycled from old railway sleepers.
far right: All the fittings, such as this door handle, are individually designed and carved.

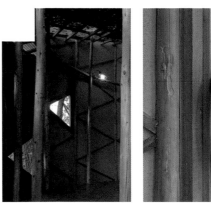

right: Double doors at the entrance. Above, cross bracing supports a sweeping roof of corrugated plastic for rain protection.

facing page: Triangular windows were fashioned by furniture craftsman Dany Nehushtai as a counterpoint to the circular form. As night falls, the circular structure becomes a lantern in the woods.

adobe mosque

In New Mexico's Abiquiu Valley, close to the house of Georgia O'Keeffe, the Dar al-Islam Mosque was designed by the Egyptian architect Hassan Fathy (1899–1989) to be built in adobe, the rammed earth building technique introduced by the Spanish to America's Southwest. Built by hand, adobe structures are the architectural equivalent of the earthen vessel, created from the mud and straw of the surrounding land. For those who live in them they impart a sense of well-being and security that derives from their natural connection with the earth, their solidity, and the soft, curving lines that result from the layers of mud applied by many hands. This natural connection is particularly appropriate for a mosque, whose positioning is important for another reason: through the direction of its prayer wall, the *qibla*, which contains the mihrab niche, it faces Mecca.

right: Triangular apertures in the adobe wall create an internal window and a triangular lattice covers the skylight above. The architect brought with him Nubian masons for the construction.

right and following pages: Load-bearing mud-brick walls carry arches that divide the interior into small domed units. Fathy spent much of his life promoting and developing mud-brick architecture.

enveloping nature

Award-winning architect Samira Rathod, based in Mumbai (Bombay), designed a weekend house in the Karjat Hills, a two-hour drive from the city, aiming not only to integrate the building with its surroundings, but also to provide the client with a meditative space amid nature. The site includes a small lake visited by waterbirds and ringed by trees, and the area for building was a small bluff dropping sharply 14 feet down to the water's edge. On her first visit, Rathod realized that the house and these natural surroundings should interpenetrate. For the single bedroom she designed a balcony that not only projects into the mid-levels of the trees, but is divided from the room by only a sliding glass partition that hangs from a ceiling rail and so allows a seamless extension of the red sandstone flooring. For the client, it is "a place under the tree," and the species is, appropriately enough, the *bodhi* tree, Ficus religiosa, the tree of enlightenment.

facing page: With the hanging glass partitions opened, the room projects out into the *bodhi* tree.

In India, meditation pre-dated Buddhism, and combined with yoga was one of the ancient Vedic sciences. One of the most auspicious places for meditation is Rishikesh, where the river Ganges finally leaves the Himalayas; in Hinduism it is believed that meditation here leads to the attainment of salvation. High above the river is the palace of the maharaja of Tehri Garhwal, on the grounds of which the spa and yoga center of Ananda has been created.

far right: Sunrise, with the outliers of the Himalayas behind the open pavilion.
right: Sunset meditation on the raised dais of the pavilion, in front of the reflecting pool.

At the south end of the palace lawn, surrounded by a water pool, is an open marble pavilion used for yogic meditation classes. In meditation, breathing is an important technique. Breath is life, and is also the origin of qi (see page 173). Here, as the instructors tell students, you inhale and exhale the pure, cool air of the Himalayas and connect with the mountains.

devi garh

An eighteenth-century Rajasthani fort, long abandoned, became the subject of an imaginative restoration in the late 1990s, when the owner, Lekha Poddar, decided to turn it into a luxury resort hotel. Typical in many ways of Indian forts, Devi Garh was a multistoried, self-contained world, with a commanding hilltop position overlooking the Aravali Hills. Because the conversion allowed for no more than thirty suites, there was no pressure on space, and the upper level of the ramparts is used for yoga and meditation at sunrise. This area of the fort includes several small enclosed balconies that project out from the high walls, known as *zharookha*. The three small walls are in the form of carved, perforated stone screens, or *jali*, that allow air and light but offer a measure of protection.

far right: A mattress and bolsters in front of an arched niche on the upper terrace.
right: A small hanging balcony projecting from high on one of the walls of the fort.

grotto

Water plays an essential role in Hinduism in general (the Sanskrit word for pilgrimage site is *tirtha*, meaning a ford across a river) and in the special form of the religion in Bali in particular. Water is a divine gift that feeds the rice terraces cut into the hills and valleys of this mountainous island, and the Balinese call their religion, which developed from traditional Indian Hinduism along idiosyncratic lines, *Agama Tirtha*, or "Science of the Sacred Water." Close to the town of Ubud, on the outskirts of Batuan village, the Bali Purnati Center for the Arts was established in 1999 as a cultural foundation for Indonesian arts, a facility for workshops and performances. Directly below the performance theater is a *beji*, or sacred spring, set within a grotto that has long been a natural, isolated spot for meditation.

below: The water eventually flows into the stream that ultimately feeds some of Bali's countless rice terraces.

right: Fed by underground springs, water wells up at the base of a rock overhang to fill a small, still pool.

theatrum botanicum

The Cartier Foundation for Contemporary Arts opened in 1994 at its new exhibition space in Paris. While the exhibitions in the large transparent building change regularly, the grounds themselves are a permanent art installation by the German artist Lothar Baumgarten. Plantings of flowers, herbs, and grasses extend back from the building toward a gently rising, terraced slope. Baumgarten consulted the medieval catalogues known as *Theatrum Botanicum* that describe medicinal and edible aromatic plants, hence the name. Set into the slope, three flights of steps lead down from different directions into a sunken oval space of pale stone. The wild garden around the exhibition building is already a rural retreat from the busy city, but descending to the miniature amphitheater, overhung with trees on one side, takes the visitor far away, into a place built for the contemplation of nature.

The furnishings are minimal: two simple stone benches and a water trough follow the curve of the wall.

facing page, top: Sunk into the slope that rises behind the foundation, the oval meditation space is entered by three stone staircases.

facing page, bottom: Surrounded by trees but below ground level, the space isolates the senses from the noise and presence of the city.

phytolab

Award-winning French designer Matali Crasset looked for her inspiration in the bathroom, to which this "experiential space" is devoted. She believes that "the bath constitutes a privileged moment of connection to one's own body, in terms of hygiene and aesthetics." The space she created, called *Phytolab*, gives substance to this holistic view by enclosing it with a hundred plants set in acrylic, so that the user can also "bathe in chlorophyll." The room within a room is built of square acrylic plates joined at the corners, each with a hole in the center into which an individual plant pot fits. According to Crasset, "the plant presses up against both sides of the wall. There is no longer any relation to planet earth, to extraterrestrial cultures. You breathe. You smell the freshness of the scent of chlorophyll." The user is intended to choose the plants, to know their aromatic and therapeutic values, and to use them in the bath or as infusions. "Here you can concoct your own compositions with all the plant species at your disposal," she explains.

facing page: A room within a room, Crasset's *Phytolab* extends the idea of the bath into a space defined by plant life.

temple trees

The approach to a tea-ceremony room is a transitional space, normally in the form of a path through a garden, which prepares visitors, for the passage from the profane world to the pure. At Yojuin temple, founded in 1244 in the old castle town of Kawagoe, it was decided to build a modern architectural form of tea-ceremony room. From over seven hundred entries, the design chosen was that of Ken Yokogawa, in which the major part of the structure is devoted to

right: Viewed from one end of the partially open structure, the alignment of trees and concrete walls lead toward the room.

the approach. A series of overlapping short walls in bare, polished concrete, and an outer frame of slatted red cedar partially enclose the old zelkova and gingko trees, which are allowed to grow through the structure by means of circular openings in the roof. Shallow reflecting ponds filled with black pebbles are separated by a crosswalk of travertine marble and beds of white pebbles. Near the center is a curved bench of Brazilian hardwood. Yokogawa calls

this a "terminus space," because its purpose is to be not just a passageway but also a place for waiting and communing with the trees and their surroundings.

right: The waiting bench, in hardwood and stainless steel, sited where the travertine walkway begins.

right: At the far end of the structure, a short series of stepping stones leads to the low, small entrance of the tea-ceremony room, set in an aluminum wall.

humble wood

Terunobu Fujimori, whose two rooms supported by cut trees (room on a perch on pages 98–103 and tree-top on pages 212–217) are part of a body of work that is a highly individual reaction to mainstream modernism, built his own house in Tokyo with studied rustic simplicity. In the center on the ground floor, he indulged himself with a spacious *washitsu*, the traditionally spare, lightly furnished room that is almost always floored with tatami mats made of *igusa* straw. Here, however, he diverged and laid split-bamboo matting without divisions for a more austere effect. For the walls and ceiling he used roughly hewn wood planking, the uneven gaps between them filled with a white plaster into which he mixed shavings and short stalks of straw. Two windows flood the room with daylight—the opposite of the dim, shadowy atmosphere that traditionally pervades such spaces.

right: Planking covers the walls and ceiling of the *washitsu*, and split-bamboo matting blankets the floor.

firewood and plaster

This tiny vaulted room is recognizably another Terunobu Fujimori design, though unexpectedly a form of tea-ceremony room. It is part of an unusual house that won the Japan Art Grand Prix in 1997 for Fujimori, who built it for a friend, the renowned artist and novelist Genpei Akasegawa. The two devised a wooden house that incorporates nature in odd ways, not the least being a thousand Chinese chives growing in individually watered pots embed-ded in the roof. Protruding from this gently sloping, wide roof, Fujimori devised this space, which can be accessed only with some difficulty via a narrow passage under the eaves. The roof is its key feature, a vault of firewood. Fujimori and Akesegawa decided to have a "roof-raising," and on one appointed day a group of friends arrived and com-pleted the room from a stack of firewood.

right: A vaulted roof of ordinary firewood over a simple, roughly plastered interior. A banana plant takes the place of more sophis-ticated flower arrangements.

In another foray into the world of the woods, Fujimori decided in 2000 to build himself a "hideout in the treetops." The idea came when he was designing the room perched on the fork of a chestnut tree on pages 98–103, and he found that he wanted to take this basic form still further. He was not interested in building an actual tree house in a living tree, but wanted more of a "hut on stilts." Once, on the summit of a Mayan temple in Yucatán, Mexico, he had realized the specialness of being above the surrounding rain forest. "I was made to realize the 'holiness' of the observer's eye looking down on the ocean of trees." The site he chose for the hut was a plot owned by his parents in the wooded hills of Chino, where he grew up. The original plan was for a floor height of 33 feet, but he realized that 20 feet would be safer and more practical. The roof, nevertheless, reaches 33 feet high.

He selected two chestnut trees to be cut from the local communal forest, each 26 feet tall and 12 inches in diameter. These were sunk 5 feet into the ground, stabilized with a poured concrete base, and tested for their load-bearing capacity. Fujimori assembled his usual group of friends, the "Jomon Kenchiku-dan" (an architectural society with a special interest in old traditions), to help him in the construction, which took from the fall of 2003 until June 2004. The floor area is a little less than 54 square feet, and the roof is sheathed in handmade corrugated copper plates.

facing page: Perched high among the pines in Nagano Prefecture, the hideout sways with the breeze. Access is via a 20-foot ladder and a push-up hatch in the floor.
right: Inside, the white plastered interior rises to a pyramidal ceiling with a gilded skylight.

The plastered white interior includes a hearth and chimney, and windows on three sides that look out over the fields, woodlands, and the mountains of Shinshu.

The hut wobbles as you climb up into it and sways in the breeze, but this simply reinforces its oneness with the surrounding treetops. It is furnished with extreme simplicity and can function as a tea-ceremony room, as a hideaway in which to relax, and as a place for writing. Fujimori named it Takasugian, "the too-high room."

above left: Two of the three windows look out over the valley and mountains. In the far corner is a hearth with an opening to a small chimney above.

above right: The projecting skylight at the apex of the roof is lined with gold leaf applied by Fujimori's father, Hisao, to "catch the reflection of the afternoon sun," even if he does comment that "Terunobu's made one of his strange things again!"

above: The construction of the room is cedar planking, rendered with plaster. One of the chestnut trunks has been allowed to protrude through the wall.

right: Built with the help of friends and students, the "too-high room" cost around two million yen (19,000 U.S. dollars) and took nine months to build.

pyramid

When advertising creative director Yoshiaki Kobayashi commissioned interior designer Yasuo Kondo to build him a new house, he added an important specification—that it include a meditative space which he could use to generate creative ideas. Kobayashi knew that his best work came quietly, away from the office environment, and often late at night. Kondo, whose other works include many of fashion designer Yohji Yamamoto's shops and the Tokyo Stock Exchange, had a unique solution: to build what he called a "house in a house"—an energizing space that borrowed one of the principles of the traditional Japanese Buddhist temple dome, the *o-do*. In the same way that a pyramid is believed by many to concentrate energy and aid meditation, the o-do is felt to aid a priest's concentration. However, this being a house in space-conscious residential Tokyo, Kondo and his client planned for dual use. In the center of the house, the living room was extended vertically into a pyramid, the apex of which reaches the roof and is a skylight. Practically, this meant projecting through the upper story of the house, in effect losing a potential room. However, Kobayashi gained a calm, white space with natural energy which, as he describes it, is completely sealed off from the world.

facing page: A row of small windows halfway up brings in light from the upper floor, and the skylight at the apex of the pyramid opens through the roof of the house.
right: Part of the upper floor is occupied by the pyramid, which is passed by a narrow corridor.

glass tent

Using one of the archetypes for shelter as a constructional model, British artist Rosie Leventon designed this conelike structure in glass and aluminum as "an easily portable, moveable personal space." With resonances of the tepee of the Plains Indians, *Light Sleeper* uses aluminum poles fastened together at the top, their bases spread out as a frame on which are hung hundreds of small sheets of glass connected with wire. For Leventon, glass holds a strange quality: "It seems to be simultaneously there but scarcely visible, like water that has solidified." The quasi-pyramidal shape allows energy to accumulate for the user, and provides a perceptual space that hovers between reality and imagination. This indeed is the subtext of this glass tent: it is designed to promote a meditation on vulnerability and on the illusion of solidity and permanence in life, one of the continuing themes in Leventon's work. The shelter that this space provides is in one sense a thin layer of security that can easily be shattered, yet there is also a perceptual protection from which the mind can draw strength.

facing page: *Light Sleeper*, with its delicate skin of glass, erected in a park under the shade of a chestnut tree.
right: The extent to which the tent encloses varies with the light falling on it. Looking out from the shade, it appears almost completely transparent.

above: Used for meditation, the tent becomes a place "for personal energy to accumulate."

facing page: The fabric of the tent is constructed from small cut squares of glass, with drilled holes at the corners linked with wire.

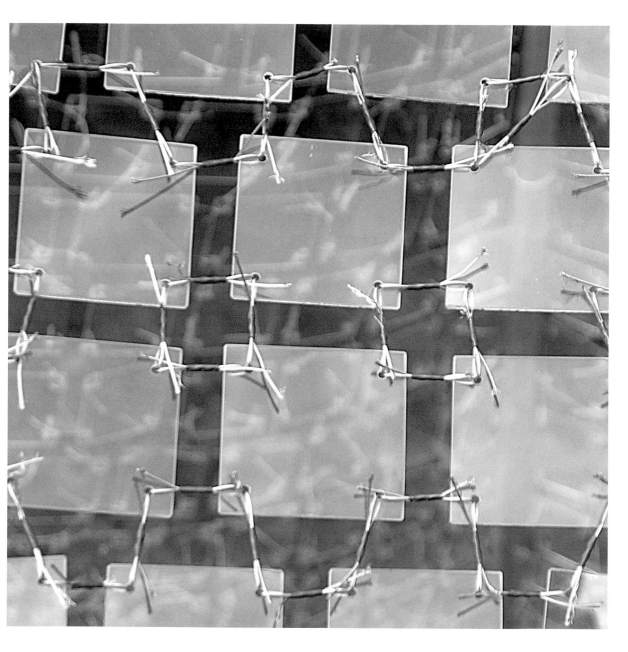

pavilions for reflection

The gardens of Suzhou in China's Jiangsu Province represent possibly the greatest concentration of spaces designed to the Chinese scholar's aesthetic. Built mainly in the Ming and Qing dynasties, they are refined constructions for strolling, sitting, and above all contemplating, as names such as the Garden of Quiet Meditation and the Retreat and Reflection Garden indicate. In particular, they embody the philosophical concepts of Confucianism, Taoism, and Buddhism. Many techniques were employed to manipulate space and its experience and to provide a meditative quality. These included a considered use of water, both as a spatial element and for reflections, the creation of miniature gardens within the garden, a folded layout of paths to maximize the number of different views, and "borrowed landscape"— making distant elements, such as a far pagoda, seem to be a part of the garden. At judiciously selected locations within each garden, pavilions were sited so that, seated inside, one is presented with a view that has been chosen and framed by the designer.

Sitting in silence
I enter in deep meditation
the still pond
calms my emotions
from afar
—a Suzhou garden plaque

facing page: The roof and pillars of a pavilion at the garden of Zhuozheng Yuan, where willow branches frame a view that uses water reflections to create an atmosphere of calm and contemplation.
right: Walkways cross a pond. The designer used the layout of paths to control the way in which the space was to be experienced.

above: A pavilion strategically sited at Zhuozheng Yuan, seen here in the early morning.

facing page: Framing extends to small, precise views of plantings created through differently shaped windows, here at the Liu Yuan garden.

cylinder

Geometric simplicity and unpainted concrete in the Brutalist manner are hallmarks of the work of Japan's respected architect Tadao Ando, and with this vocabulary he has continued many of the traditions of Japanese architecture by designing buildings which, in the words of architectural historian Kenneth Frampton, "express a sense of contemplation and meditation in both form and material." One of the most directly expressive is Ando's Meditation Space, completed in 1995 for the UNESCO headquarters in Paris to commemorate its fiftieth anniversary. A 21-foot-high cylinder in reinforced concrete, it opens through two plain, facing doorways onto concrete walkways, while inside light filters down from the circumference of a floating concrete disc. The simplicity, almost anonymity, of the cylinder is an attempt to transcend culture to make a place of meditation "for all peoples of the world" and to symbolize peace. Less obvious is the flooring, which is granite from the city of Hiroshima that was exposed to radiation from the atomic bomb dropped on August 6, 1945; the cleaned stone is used inside the cylinder and in the artificial pond outside.

facing page: The cylinder and its reflecting pond, in the center of the UNESCO complex.
right: A raised concrete path bisects the austerely finished Meditation Space.

above: A 270-degree panorama shows the interior, furnished simply with four chairs. The walls are occasionally used for art exhibitions.

facing page: The floating ceiling is smaller than the full diameter to function as a skylight.

divine wind

Of all cultures that recognize natural spiritual energy, Japan has formalized it the most, as Shinto. Since ancient times, the Japanese have acknowledged the existence of spiritual beings, or *kami*, within all aspects of nature. The shrines have the direct simplicity of natural materials that include a sacred cypress (*hinoki*), bamboo, bark, and thatch. The basis of Shinto faith is the consciousness of harmony and unity between human beings and nature, and the shrines are places where, through quiet contemplation, this can be reaffirmed. They are built afresh every twenty years, identically and without change, and have been since the fifth century, making them both new and unchanging at the same time.

The most sacred of all Shinto shrines are the two at Isé, on the Mie Peninsula. The main outer sanctuary, Geku, is devoted to the kami Toyouke, and the shrine, in keeping with the status of the deity, is concealed, enclosed by four rows of fences, and yet, not totally concealed. Worshippers and visitors may approach only as far as the first gate, in front of which hangs a plain white curtain; if the breeze catches it, the curtain will lift briefly for the patient observer. Appropriately enough, and with a gentler meaning than its usual resonance in the West, this stirring of the air in front of the shrine is the "divine wind," or *kamikaze*.

right: As the air stirs in front of the shrine, a corner of the concealing curtain rises for a moment.

kinetic space

The brief flowering of Kinetic Art in the mid-1960s produced a handful of serious artists whose aim was to use movement, either actual or implied, as a means of representing larger natural forces, making the nonvisual material. Among them, Liliane Lijn worked on transforming scientific principles into art. The culmination of several years of experimentation with acrylic, light, and water, inspired by her interest in astronomy and the physics of light, was

this construction, *Liquid Reflections*, which occupies a small, darkened room. In its center, a hollow acrylic disc containing water revolves on a spotlit, motorized turntable. Two acrylic balls rotate on the surface, their motion subject to opposing forces: the centrifugal force of the spin of the disc and the centripetal due to the concavity of the disc surface. The surrounding black cubic interior remains just visible beyond this constant movement.

facing page: The spotlit, rotating disc sits in a blackened cubic room, only just visible to the observer as the kinetic scene unfolds in the center.
right: On the underside of the surface on which the acrylic spheres move, water that has been introduced into the hollow disc evaporates and condenses in a constantly changing film of droplets.

As Lijn describes it: "When first poured into the disc, the water condenses into patterns which resemble interstellar clouds of gas, but soon contracts into precise spherical droplets, alive and trembling, which in turn become increasingly homogeneous covering the entire surface of the disc. The water in the disc both influences the total equilibrium and is influenced by it, while the movement of the balls on its surface follows the laws of momen-

tum. They also act as moving magnifying lenses, bringing to life now one area of the disc, now another with a strange lunar landscape of reflections and shadows. This is my attempt on an intimate scale to contemplate the universe." The series is in many public collections, including The Museum of Modern Art in New York and Tate Britain in London, where it appeared in the major 2004 retrospective of art of the '60s, *This Was Tomorrow*.

above and facing page: The two spheres perform a kind of cosmic dance as they continually collide and separate across the gently concave, slowly spinning surface.

following pages: Refracting and concentrating the light, the spheres act like moving lenses to illuminate the surface and underside of the disc.

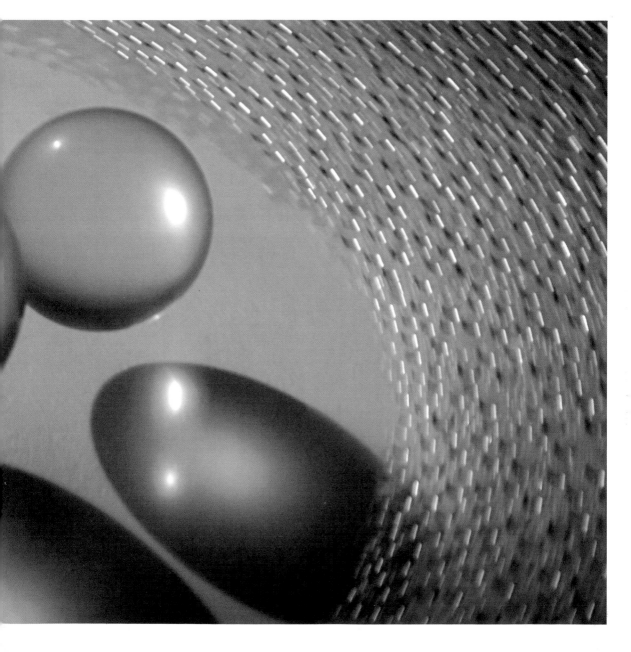

acknowledgments

Genpei Akasegawa
Atsushi Akenuki
Hitoshi Akino
Ananda resort
Tadao Ando
Yasujirou Aoki
Asia Society, New York
Bali Purnati Center
    For The Arts
Beacon Communications
Lothar Baumgarten
Cartier Foundation for
Contemporary Arts
Chris Cook
Matali Crasset
Dynamic Tools Corporation
FOBA architects
Takao Fujiki
Terunobu Fujimori
Sarah Gillham
Tetsuo Goto
Yukio Hashimoto
Masahiro Hasui
Kunihiko Hayakawa
Bernard Hermann
Takuto Hiki
Hofu Crematorium
Icehotel
Masatochi Izumi
Shinji Kagawa
Akira Kaho
Sangita Kathiwada
Mr & Mrs Kato
Michimasa Kawaguchi
Chitoshi Kihara
Roland Kirishima
Atsushi Kitagawara

Klein Dytham architects
Yoshiaki Kobayashi
Yasuo Kondo
Kojimachi Kaikan
Katsumata family
Kengo Kuma
Masahisa & Tsuneko Koike
Yuuichi Kurosawa
Danny Lane
Rosie Leventon
Liliane Lijn
Leonard Lueras
Hansjörg Mayer
    and Mimi Lipton
Shunmyo Masuno
Mikami Architects
Yuko Minamide
Amon Miyamoto
Kamal Morarka
Takeshi Nagasaki
Dany Nehushtai
Opus Arisugawa
Lekha and Ranjan Poddar
Samira Rathod
Samye monastery
Yukako Shibata
Toshihiko Suzuki
Jun Tamaki
Mr & Mrs Tanaka
Tate Britain
Toriumi family
UNESCO
Anne Wood
Takashi Yamaguchi
Ken Yokogawa
Tatsuhiko Yokoo